THE ANSWERING VOICE

LOVE LYRICS BY WOMEN

THE ANSWERING VOICE

LOVE LYRICS BY WOMEN

SELECTED BY
SARA TEASDALE

NEW EDITION
With Fifty Recent Poems Added

Granger Index Reprint Series

BOOKS FOR LIBRARIES PRESS
FREEPORT, NEW YORK

AAN 5090

INTERNATIONAL STANDARD BOOK NUMBER:
0-8369-6323-7

LIBRARY OF CONGRESS CATALOG CARD NUMBER:
76-37023

PRINTED IN THE UNITED STATES OF AMERICA
BY
NEW WORLD BOOK MANUFACTURING CO., INC.
HALLANDALE, FLORIDA 33009

THE HAPPY LABOR
OF SELECTING THESE POEMS
I DEDICATE TO
MY SISTER

*Ἔρος δαὖτέ μ' ὁ λυσιμέλης δόνει
γλυκύπικρον ἀμάχανον ὄρπετον.*

" *O gods, what love, what yearning, contributed to
this.*"

FOREWORD

THE decade since 1917 has produced more good poetry by women than any other in the history of our language. In saying this I am not forgetting the three remarkable women poets of the last century. Christina Rossetti and Emily Dickinson were born within five days of each other. Elizabeth Barrett Browning was nearly twenty-five years their senior. But it was not until 1890, long after the work of the other two had become a recognized part of our literary heritage, that Emily Dickinson's poems appeared.

In contrast to the lapse of time between 1820, when Elizabeth Barrett's first book was published, and the end of the century, when Emily Dickinson's first volume appeared, our own decade is strangely fortunate. It has seen the full flowering of two women poets of very high rank, and of a dozen others not unworthy to be considered with them. One must go back to Sappho's time, perhaps, to find another brief period equally rich. It would be a pleasant task to gather certain of the most perfect phrases and single lines from the work of to-day, and set them apart so as to compare their intensity with that older beauty. It may be that the fragments spared us by the centuries owe a part of their magic to their isolation, to the fact that our imaginations make from these few vivid far-strewn petals, flowers more beautiful than ever have existed in reality.

But whether or not contemporary poems would stand this test, it is undeniable that a new impetus has been given to women to express themselves in poetry. The work of to-day differs so radically in feeling from the work of twenty-five years ago as to furnish the clue to the reason for the unusual amount of verse written. Women have been forced to write because they found nothing to hand that expressed their thoughts.

Though the passion called love has not changed appreciably during recorded time, our ideas about it have changed constantly, and sometimes with great rapidity. The immediate cause of the new attitude may be traced to the growing economic independence of women consequent on education, and to the universal tendency to rationalize all emotion.

The poems in the second part of this book have been selected in a leisurely way during several years. I had only one thought in gathering them together, to take what seemed to me the best contemporary love poems by women. It was not until after the selection had been made that I realized fully the change of mood which distinguishes the later from the earlier part of the book, a change as striking as is felt when an orchestra stills its wood-winds and attacks a vigorous passage for strings. Or, to vary the figure, the difference might be typified by the change in women's costumes during the past quarter of a century — so spare, so restrained as to ornament, so casual are they to-day in comparison with the amplitude, the elaborateness, the formality of that other time. Though the material be no richer now, the result is more to our present taste, more compatible with movement and open air.

FOREWORD

There is a wider range of feeling as well as a less conventional treatment in contemporary poetry. One finds little now of that ingratiating dependence upon the beloved, those vows of eternal and unwavering adoration, which filled the poems of even the sincerest women of the times before our own. One finds little, too, of the pathetic despair so often present in the earlier work. To-day there is stated over and over, perhaps at times overstated, the woman's fearlessness, her love of change, her almost cruelly analytical attitude. The strident or flippant notes that occasionally mar the poems, arise from overstating new ideas, a habit that seems unavoidable until through long possession they have become unselfconscious. This is a period of transition. The perfect balance between the heart and the mind, the body and the spirit, is still to be attained.

If, in adding as many as fifty poems to represent this comparatively short period, I lay myself open to criticism, I can say only that our own times are rightly more interesting to us than any other, and that they are indubitably rich.

Foreword

It is to be regretted that several poets whose work in other subjects is notable, have written few or no love poems. This is true of the English poets Sylvia Lynd and Fredegond Shove, and of the American poet, Marianne Moore. Because of the desire to confine the new section to not more than fifty poems, it was necessary to omit the work of many of the women still writing who are represented in the earlier part of the book. Those in the first part who appear also in the second, I have regretfully restricted to one poem each.

Sara Teasdale

New York, April, 1928.

PREFATORY NOTE TO THE
FIRST EDITION

I HAVE tried to bring together in this book the most beautiful love-lyrics written in English by women since the middle of the last century. During this period, for the first time in the history of English literature, the work of women has compared favorably with that of men; and in no other field have they done such noteworthy work as in poetry. Before this period, for reasons well known to the student of feminism, sincere love poems by women were very rare in England and America. With the exception of Lady Barnard's " Auld Robin Gray " and a poem by Susanna Blamire, I have found nothing that seemed worthy of inclusion.

In most cases the finest utterance of women poets has been on love, so that this book is, I venture to hope, a golden treasury of lyrics by women.

I have included no long poems, and no translations, and I have avoided poems in which the poet dramatized a man's feelings rather than her own.

I want to acknowledge very gratefully my in-

Prefatory Note

debtedness for counsel and suggestions to Harriet
Monroe, Jessie B. Rittenhouse, Louis Untermeyer,
Henry L. Mencken, William Stanley Braithwaite,
Thomas S. Jones, Jr., John Hall Wheelock, and
Thomas B. Mosher. From my husband, Ernst B.
Filsinger, I have received unfailing aid and encour-
agement.

Sara Teasdale

New York, April, 1917.

CONTENTS

PART ONE

APOLOGY. *Amy Lowell* 27

APRIL GHOST, AN. *Lizette Woodworth Reese* . . 102

ASHES OF LIFE. *Edna St. Vincent Millay* . . . 70

AULD ROBIN GRAY. *Anne Barnard* 104

"BELOVÈD, MY BELOVÈD, WHEN I THINK." *Elizabeth Barrett Browning* 26

BIRCH TREE AT LOSCHWITZ, THE. *Amy Levy* . . 2

BIRTHDAY, A. *Christina Rossetti* 17

CARNATIONS. *Margaret Widdemer* 97

CHOICE. *Emily Dickinson* 19

"COME BACK TO ME." *Christina Rossetti* . . . 69

COMRADES. *Fannie Stearns Davis* 49

CONNAUGHT LAMENT, A. *Nora Chesson* . . . 10

"CUTTIN' RUSHES." *Moira O'Neill* 94

CYNIC, THE. *Theodosia Garrison* 72

DEBTS. *Jessie B. Rittenhouse* 46

DEEP-SEA PEARL, THE. *Edith M. Thomas* . . 103

DIRGE. *Adelaide Crapsey* 100

"DOUGLAS, DOUGLAS, TENDER AND TRUE." *Dinah Mulock Craik* 114

ECSTASY. *Sarojini Naidu* 35

xvii

Contents — Part One

Enchanted Sheep-fold, The. *Josephine Preston Peabody* 15

Farewell, A. *Harriet Monroe* 66

Finis. *Rosamund Marriott Watson* 107

Found. *Josephine Preston Peabody* 18

Friendship after Love. *Ella Wheeler Wilcox* . 84

From a Car-Window. *Ruth Guthrie Harding* . . 91

Gifts. *Juliana Horatia Ewing* 57

"Go from me." *Elizabeth Barrett Browning* . . 64

"Grandmither, think not I forget." *Willa Sibert Cather* 108

Great Man, The. *Eunice Tietjens* 37

Hawthorn Tree, The. *Willa Sibert Cather* . . 34

Heart's Country, The. *Florence Wilkinson* . . 23

"How do I love thee?" *Elizabeth Barrett Browning* 43

I am the Wind. *Zoë Akins* 80

"I have wandered to a spring." *Edna Wahlert McCourt* 5

I know. *Elsa Barker* 39

"I leaned out my window." *Jean Ingelow* . . 31

"I must not yield." *Nora May French* . . . 63

"I sat among the green leaves." *Marjorie L. C. Pickthall* 13

"I will not give thee all my heart." *Grace Hazard Conkling* 56

"If thou must love me, let it be for nought." *Elizabeth Barrett Browning* 41

xviii

Contents — Part One

In Deep Places. *Amelia Josephine Burr* . . . 51

In the Park. *Helen Hoyt* 14

Incantation, An. *Marguerite Wilkinson* . . . 21

Insufficiency. *Elizabeth Barrett Browning* . . 62

Land o' the Leal, The. *Carolina, Lady Nairne* . 123

"Less than the dust." *Laurence Hope* . . . 119

"Love came back at fall o' dew." *Lizette Wood-worth Reese* 90

Love is a Terrible Thing. *Grace Fallow Norton* . 8

Love me at Last. *Alice Corbin* 6

Love Song. *Mary Carolyn Davies* 22

Love Song. *Harriet Monroe* 59

Love's Change. *Anne Reeve Aldrich* 67

Lynmouth Widow, A. *Amelia Josephine Burr* . 118

Man, The. *Helen Hay Whitney* 121

Man with a Hammer, The. *Anna Wickham* . . 36

"Many in aftertimes will say." *Christina Rossetti* 78

Menace. *Katharine Tynan* 58

Message, The. *Margaret Sackville* 85

Name, The. *Williamina Parrish* 30

Norah. *Zoë Akins* 120

"Oh, the burden, the burden of love ungiven." *Grace Fallow Norton* 12

Old Song, An. *Fannie Stearns Davis* 54

Other, The. *Ethna Carbery* 86

Contents — Part One

Parting. *Emily Dickinson* 53

Parting. *Alice Freeman Palmer* 83

Passer-by, The. *Edith M. Thomas* 111

Possession. *Jean Starr Untermeyer* 60

Rain. *Jean Starr Untermeyer* 29

Rain, Rain! *Zoë Akins* 33

Rainbow, The. *Vine Colby* 88

Red May. *A. Mary F. Robinson* 7

Remembrance. *Emily Brontë* 125

Reminiscence, A. *Amy Levy* 99

Renouncement. *Alice Meynell* 65

Requiescat. *Rosamund Marriott Watson* . . . 113

Rest. *Irene Rutherford McLeod* 40

Rhapsody. *Florence Earle Coates* 24

Rispetto, i, ii, iii. *A. Mary F. Robinson* . 75, 76, 77

Sea Song. *Laurence Hope* 73

Service. *Anna Hempstead Branch* 81

Siller Crown, The. *Susanna Blamire* . . . 92

"So beautiful you are, indeed." *Irene Rutherford McLeod* 20

Somewhere or Other. *Christina Rossetti* . . 1

Taxi, The. *Amy Lowell* 44

That Day you came. *Lizette Woodworth Reese* . 52

Tired Woman, The. *Anna Wickham* 42

To a Late Comer. *Julia C. R. Dorr* 96

xx

Contents — Part One

To one Unknown. *Helen Dudley* 3

"To-day I went among the mountain folk."
Olive Tilford Dargan 101

"Under dusky laurel leaf." *Margaret Widdemer* 122

Unfulfilled. *Corinne Roosevelt Robinson* . . . 117

Unwedded. *Ada Foster Murray* 116

Vos non Vobis. *Edith M. Thomas* 11

"When I am dead." *Christina Rossetti* . . . 112

"When on the marge of evening." *Louise Imo-
gen Guiney* 25

When plaintively and near the cricket sings.
Nora May French 68

"When we shall be dust." *Muna Lee* . . . 79

Woman's Question, A. *Adelaide Anne Procter* . 47

"Yet for one rounded moment." *Edith Wharton* 61

"You say there is no love." *Grace Fallow Norton* 45

CONTENTS

PART TWO

A Memory. *Lola Ridge* 163

A Song for my Mate. *Marguerite Wilkinson* . 188

Ballad of the Rag-Bag Heart. *Marjorie Allen Seiffert* 168

Before you Came. *Marjorie Meeker* . . . 148

Benvenuto's Valentine. *Elinor Wylie* . . . 197

By the Lake. *Edith Sitwell* 143

Cherish you then the Hope I shall Forget. *Edna St. Vincent Millay* 133

Dawn. *Frances Cornford* 185

Diagonals. *Aline Kilmer* 170

Elaine. *Edna St. Vincent Millay* 152

Established. *Rose O'Neill* 160

Evadne. *H. D.* 201

His First Love. *Lizette Woodworth Reese* . . 144

Homage. *Helen Hoyt* 189

I do remember You. *Roberta Teale Swartz* . . 164

I have been through the Gates. *Charlotte Mew* 166

In the Orchard. *Muriel Stuart* 155

Contents — Part Two

LAKE-SONG. *Jean Starr Untermeyer* 205

LIKE A CLOUD, LIKE A MIST. *Helen Hoyt* . . 129

LOVE SONG FROM NEW ENGLAND. *Winifred Welles* 172

MARRIAGE. *Babette Deutsch* 196

MEN LOVED WHOLLY BEYOND WISDOM. *Louise Bogan* 154

PAGEANT. *Margaret Widdemer* 159

PARTING AFTER A QUARREL. *Eunice Tietjens* . 146

RELEASE. *Margaret Tod Ritter* 145

SEA LOVE. *Charlotte Mew* 134

SEQUENCE. *Elinor Wylie* 131

SHE SAYS, BEING FORBIDDEN. *Leonora Speyer* . 182

SONG. *Louise Bogan* 162

SONG FOR UNBOUND HAIR. *Genevieve Taggard* . 173

SONG OF THE LONG RIVER. *Constance Lindsay Skinner* 202

ST. CLARE HEARS ST. FRANCIS. *Sarah N. Cleghorn* 149

THANKS TO MY WORLD FOR THE LOAN OF A FAIR DAY. *Stella Benson* 186

THE ANCIENT BEAUTIFUL THINGS. *Fannie Stearns Davis* 191

THE DROWNÈD LOVER. *Lady Margaret Sackville* . 135

THE FARMER'S WIFE. *Martha Ostenso* . . . 175

THE HAUNTED HEART. *Jessie B. Rittenhouse* . . 147

THE ISLANDS. *H. D.* 176

xxiii

Contents — Part Two

The Letter. *Amy Lowell* 161

The Love-Song. *Bernice Lesbia Kenyon* . . . 183

The Maid's Tragedy. *Sylvia Townsend Warner* . 151

The Meeting. *Katherine Mansfield* 199

The Snow-Gardens. *Zoë Akins* 140

The Unfaithful. *Genevieve Taggard* . . . 167

To ———. *Muriel Stuart* 165

Twilit Revelation. *Léonie Adams* 138

Two Lovers. *Aline Kilmer* 137

Velvet Shoes *Elinor Wylie* 139

What Lips my Lips have Kissed. *Edna St. Vincent Millay* 204

You make me think of Loops of Water Lying. *Grace Hazard Conkling* 171

PART ONE

THE ANSWERING VOICE

SOMEWHERE OR OTHER

SOMEWHERE or other there must surely be
   The face not seen, the voice not heard,
The heart that not yet — never yet — ah, me!
   Made answer to my word.

Somewhere or other, maybe near or far;
   Past land and sea, clean out of sight;
Beyond the wandering moon, beyond the star
   That tracks her night by night.

Somewhere or other, maybe far or near;
   With just a wall, a hedge, between;
With just the last leaves of the dying year
   Fallen on a turf grown green.

                   Christina Rossetti

THE BIRCH TREE AT LOSCHWITZ

At Loschwitz above the city
  The air is sunny and chill;
The birch trees and the pine trees
  Grow thick upon the hill.

Lone and tall, with silver stem,
  A birch tree stands apart;
The passionate wind of spring-time
  Stirs in its leafy heart.

I lean against the birch tree,
  My arms around it twine;
It pulses, and leaps, and quivers,
  Like a human heart to mine.

One moment I stand, then sudden
  Let loose mine arms that cling:
O God! the lonely hillside,
  The passionate wind of spring!

Amy Levy

2

TO ONE UNKNOWN

I HAVE seen the proudest stars
That wander on through space,
Even the sun and moon,
But not your face.

I have heard the violin,
The winds and waves rejoice
In endless minstrelsy;
Yet not your voice.

I have touched the trillium,
Pale flower of the land,
Coral, anemone,
And not your hand.

I have kissed the shining feet
Of Twilight lover-wise,
Opened the gates of Dawn —
Oh, not your eyes!

THE ANSWERING VOICE

I have dreamed unwonted things,
Visions that witches brew,
Spoken with images,
Never with you.

Helen Dudley

"I HAVE WANDERED TO A SPRING"

I HAVE wandered to a spring in the forest green
     and dim,
The sweet quiet stirs about me —
The water twinkles at me,
As I stoop to dip my cup,
    As I stoop to drink — to him.

True, I 'm only half in earnest — I touch the cool,
     wet brim —
He 'd laugh if he could see me —
I 'm glad he does n't see me,
As alone with my queer gladness,
    I stoop to drink — to him.

Edna Wahlert McCourt

LOVE ME AT LAST

Love me at last, or if you will not,
    Leave me;
Hard words could never, as these half-words,
    Grieve me:
Love me at last — or leave me.

Love me at last, or let the last word uttered
    Be but your own;
Love me, or leave me — as a cloud, a vapor,
    Or a bird flown.
Love me at last — I am but sliding water
    Over a stone.

Alice Corbin

RED MAY

OUT of the window the trees in the Square
  Are covered with crimson May —
You, that were all of my love and my care,
  Have broken my heart to-day.

But though I have lost you and though I despair
  Till even the past looks gray —
Out of the window the trees in the Square
  Are covered with crimson May.

A. Mary F. Robinson

LOVE IS A TERRIBLE THING

I WENT out to the farthest meadow,
I lay down in the deepest shadow;

And I said unto the earth, " Hold me,"
And unto the night, " O enfold me,"

And unto the wind petulantly
I cried, " You know not for you are free!"

And I begged the little leaves to lean
Low and together for a safe screen;

Then to the stars I told my tale:
" That is my home-light, there in the vale,

" And O, I know that I shall return,
But let me lie first mid the unfeeling fern.

" For there is a flame that has blown too near,
And there is a name that has grown too dear,
And there is a fear . . ."

8

Love is a Terrible Thing

And to the still hills and cool earth and far sky
        I made moan,
"The heart in my bosom is not my own!

"O would I were free as the wind on wing;
  Love is a terrible thing!"

Grace Fallow Norton

A CONNAUGHT LAMENT

I WILL arise and go hence to the west,
And dig me a grave where the hill-winds call;
But oh, were I dead, were I dust, the fall
Of my own love's footstep would break my rest!

My heart in my bosom is black as a sloe!
I heed not cuckoo, nor wren, nor swallow:
Like a flying leaf in the sky's blue hollow
The heart in my breast is, that beats so low.

Because of the words your lips have spoken,
(O dear black head that I must not follow)
My heart is a grave that is stripped and hollow,
As ice on the water my heart is broken.

O lips forgetful and kindness fickle,
The swallow goes south with you: I go west
Where fields are empty and scythes at rest.
I am the poppy and you the sickle;
My heart is broken within my breast.

Nora Chesson

10

VOS NON VOBIS

THERE was a garden planned in Spring's young
     days,
Then Summer held it in her bounteous hand,
And many wandered through its blooming ways,
But ne'er the one for whom the work was planned.
     And it was vainly done —
For what are many, if we lack the one?

There was a song that lived within the heart
Long time — and then on Music's wing it strayed!
All sing it now, all praise its artless art,
But ne'er the one for whom the song was made.
     And it was vainly done —
For what are many, if we lack the one!

Edith M. Thomas

11

"OH, THE BURDEN, THE BURDEN OF LOVE UNGIVEN"

Oh, the burden, the burden of love ungiven,
    The weight of laughter unshed,
Oh, heavy caresses, unblown tendernesses,
    Oh, love-words unsung and unsaid.

Oh, the burden, the burden of love unspoken,
    The cramp of silence close-furled,
To lips that would utter, to hands that would
        scatter
    Love's seed on the paths of the world.

Oh, the heavy burden of love ungiven:
    My breast doth this burden bear;
Deep in my bosom the unblown blossom —
    My world-love that withers there.

Grace Fallow Norton

"I SAT AMONG THE GREEN LEAVES"

I sat among the green leaves, and heard the nuts
      falling,
  The blood-red butterflies were gold against the
      sun,
But in between the silence and the sweet birds calling
  The nuts fell one by one.

Why should they fall and the year but half over?
  Why should sorrow seek me and I so young
      and kind?
The leaf is on the bough and the dew is on the clover,
  But the green nuts are falling in the wind.

Oh, I gave my lips away and all my soul behind
      them.
  Why should trouble follow and the quick tears
      start?
The little birds may love and fly with only God
      to mind them,
  But the green nuts are falling on my heart.

Marjorie L. C. Pickthall

13

IN THE PARK

HE whistled soft whistlings I knew were for me,
Teasing, endearing.
Won't you look? was what they said,
But I did not turn my head.
(Only a little I turned my hearing.)

My feet took me by;
Straight and evenly they went:
As if they had not dreamed what he meant:
As if such a curiosity
Never were known since the world began
As woman wanting man!

My heart led me past and took me away;
And yet it was my heart that wanted to stay.

Helen Hoyt

THE ENCHANTED SHEEP–FOLD

THE hills far-off were blue, blue,
  The hills at hand were brown;
And all the herd-bells called to me
  As I came by the down.

The briars turned to roses — roses,
  Ever we stayed to pull
A white little rose, and a red little rose,
  And a lock of silver wool.

Nobody heeded, — none, none;
  And when True Love came by,
They thought him nought but the shepherd-boy.
  Nobody knew but I!

The trees were feathered like birds, birds;
  Birds were in every tree.
Yet nobody heeded, nobody heard,
  Nobody knew, save we.

The Answering Voice

And he is fairer than all, — all.
  How could a heart go wrong?
For his eyes I knew, and his knew mine,
  Like an old, old song.

Josephine Preston Peabody

A BIRTHDAY

My heart is like a singing bird
    Whose nest is in a watered shoot:
My heart is like an apple tree
    Whose boughs are bent with thickset fruit;
My heart is like a rainbow shell
    That paddles in a halcyon sea;
My heart is gladder than all these
    Because my love is come to me.

Raise me a dais of silk and down;
    Hang it with vair and purple dyes;
Carve it in doves and pomegranates,
    And peacocks with a hundred eyes;
Work it in gold and silver grapes,
    In leaves and silver fleurs-de-lys;
Because the birthday of my life
    Is come, my love is come to me.

Christina Rossetti

FOUND

Oh, when I saw your eyes,
So old it was, so new, the hushed surprise:
After a long, long search, it came to be,
Home folded me.

And looking up, I saw
The far, first stars like tapers to my awe,
In the dim hands of hid, benignant Powers,
At search long hours.

And did they hear us call,
That they have found us children after all?
And did you know, O Wonderful and Dear,
That I was here?

Josephine Preston Peabody

18

CHOICE

OF all the souls that stand create
I have elected one.
When sense from spirit files away,
And subterfuge is done;

When that which is and that which was
Apart, intrinsic, stand,
And this brief tragedy of flesh
Is shifted like a sand;

When figures show their royal front
And mists are carved away, —
Behold the atom I preferred
To all the lists of clay!

Emily Dickinson

" SO BEAUTIFUL YOU ARE INDEED "

So beautiful you are, indeed,
That I am troubled when you come,
And though I crave you for my need,
Your nearness strikes me blind and dumb.

And when you bring your lips to mine
My spirit trembles and escapes,
And you and I are turned divine,
Bereft of our familiar shapes.

And fearfully we tread cold space,
Naked of flesh and winged with flame,
. . . Until we find us face to face,
Each calling on the other's name!

Irene Rutherford McLeod

20

AN INCANTATION

O STRONG sun of heaven, harm not my love,
Sear him not with your flame, blind him not with
        your beauty,
Shine for his pleasure!

O gray rains of heaven, harm not my love,
Drown not in your torrent the song of his heart,
Lave and caress him!

O swift winds of heaven, harm not my love,
Bruise not nor buffet him with your rough humor,
Sing you his prowess!

O mighty triad, strong ones of heaven,
Sun, rain and wind, be gentle, I charge you;
For your mad mood of wrath have me, I am ready—
But spare him, my lover, most proud and most
        dear —
O sun, rain and wind, strong ones of heaven!

                            Marguerite Wilkinson

21

LOVE SONG

THERE is a strong wall about me to protect me:
It is built of the words you have said to me.

There are swords about me to keep me safe:
They are the kisses of your lips.

Before me goes a shield to guard me from harm:
It is the shadow of your arms between me and
    danger.

All the wishes of my mind know your name,
And the white desires of my heart
They are acquainted with you.
The cry of my body for completeness,
That is a cry to you.
My blood beats out your name to me, unceasing,
    pitiless —
Your name, your name.

Mary Carolyn Davies

22

THE HEART'S COUNTRY

Hill people turn to their hills;
   Sea folk are sick for the sea:
Thou art my land and my country,
   And my heart calls out for thee.

The bird beats his wings for the open,
   The captive burns to be free;
But I — I cry at thy window,
   For thou art my liberty.

               Florence Wilkinson

RHAPSODY

As the mother bird to the waiting nest,
  As the regnant moon to the sea,
As joy to the heart that hath first been blest —
  So is my love to me.

Sweet as the song of the lark that soars
  From the net of the fowler free,
Sweet as the morning that song adores —
  So is my love to me!

As the rose that blossoms in matchless grace
  Where the canker may not be,
As the well that springs in a desert place —
  So is my love to me.

Florence Earle Coates

"WHEN ON THE MARGE OF EVENING"

When on the marge of evening the last blue light
    is broken,
  And winds of dreamy odor are loosened from
    afar,
Or when my lattice opens, before the lark hath
    spoken,
  On dim laburnum-blossoms, and morning's dy-
    ing star,

I think of thee (oh mine the more if other eyes
    be sleeping!)
  Whose greater noonday splendors the many
    share and see,
While sacred and forever, some perfect law is keep-
    ing
  The late, the early twilight, alone and sweet for
    me.

Louise Imogen Guiney

"BELOVÈD, MY BELOVÈD, WHEN I THINK"

BELOVÈD, my belovèd, when I think
That thou wast in the world a year ago,
What time I sat alone here in the snow,
And saw no footprint, heard the silence sink
No moment at thy voice, but link by link,
Went counting all my chains as if that so
They never could fall off at any blow
Struck by thy possible hand, — why, thus I drink
Of life's great cup of wonder! Wonderful,
Never to feel thee thrill the day or night
With personal act or speech, nor ever cull
Some prescience of thee with the blossoms white
Thou sawest growing! Atheists are as dull,
Who cannot guess God's presence out of sight.

Elizabeth Barrett Browning

APOLOGY

BE not angry with me that I bear
    Your colors everywhere,
    All through each crowded street,
      And meet
    The wonder-light in every eye,
      As I go by.

Each plodding wayfarer looks up to gaze,
    Blinded by rainbow haze,
    The stuff of happiness,
      No less,
    Which wraps me in its glad-hued folds
      Of peacock golds.

Before my feet the dusty, rough-paved way
    Flushes beneath its gray.
    My steps fall ringed with light,
      So bright,
    It seems a myriad suns are strown
      About the town.

THE ANSWERING VOICE

Around me is the sound of steepled bells,
   And rich perfumèd smells
   Hang like a wind-forgotten cloud,
     And shroud
  Me from close contact with the world.
    I dwell impearled.

You blazon me with jeweled insignia.
   A flaming nebula
   Rims in my life. And yet
     You set
  The word upon me, unconfessed
    To go unguessed.

Amy Lowell

RAIN

I HAVE always hated the rain,
And the gloom of grayed skies.
But now I think I must always cherish
Rain-hung leaf and the misty river;
And the friendly screen of dripping green
Where eager kisses were shyly given
And your pipe-smoke made clouds in our damp,
       close heaven.

The curious laggard passed us by,
His wet shoes soughed on the shining walk.
And that afternoon was filled with a blurred
       glory —
That afternoon, when we first talked as lovers.

                Jean Starr Untermeyer

THE NAME

I 'VE learned to say it carelessly,
 So no one else can see
By any little look or sign
 How dear it is to me.

But, oh, the thrill, as though you kissed
 My tingling finger-tips
Each time the golden syllables
 Fall lightly from my lips!

Williamina Parrish

"I LEANED OUT MY WINDOW"

I LEANED out my window, I smelt the white
    clover,
  Dark, dark was the garden, I saw not the gate;
Now, if there be footsteps, he comes, my one
    lover —
  Hush, nightingale, hush! Oh, sweet nightin-
    gale, wait
    Till I listen and hear
    If a step draweth near,
    For my love he is late!

"The skies in the darkness stoop nearer and nearer,
  A cluster of stars hangs like fruit in the
    tree,
The fall of the water comes sweeter, comes clearer :
  To what art thou listening, and what dost thou
    see ?
    Let the star-clusters grow,
    Let the sweet waters flow,
    And cross quickly to me.

The Answering Voice

"You night moths that hover where honey brims
        over
    From sycamore blooms, or settle or sleep;
You glowworms, shine out, and the pathway dis-
        cover
        To him that comes darkling along the rough
        steep.
            Ah, my sailor, make haste,
            For the time runs to waste,
            And my love lieth deep—

"Too deep for swift telling; and yet, my one lover,
        I 've conned thee an answer, it waits thee to-
        night."
    By the sycamore passed he, and through the white
        clover,
        Then all the sweet speech I had fashioned took
        flight;
            But I 'll love him more, more
            Than e'er wife loved before,
            Be the day dark or bright.

                                        Jean Ingelow

RAIN, RAIN!

Rain, rain, — fall, fall,
    In a heavy screen —
    That my lover be not seen!

Wind, wind, — blow, blow,
    Till the leaves are stirred —
    That my lover be not heard!

Storm, storm, — rage, rage,
    Like a war around —
    That my lover be not found!

. . . Lark, lark, — hush . . . hush . . .
    Softer music make —
    That my lover may not wake. . . .

Zoë Akins

THE HAWTHORN TREE

Across the shimmering meadows —
Ah, when he came to me!
In the spring-time,
In the night-time,
In the starlight,
Beneath the hawthorn tree.

Up from the misty marshland —
Ah, when he climbed to me!
To my white bower,
To my sweet rest,
To my warm breast,
Beneath the hawthorn tree.

Ask of me what the birds sang,
High in the hawthorn tree;
What the breeze tells,
What the rose smells,
What the stars shine —
Not what he said to me!

Willa Sibert Cather

ECSTASY

Cover mine eyes, O my Love!
  Mine eyes that are weary of bliss
As of light that is poignant and strong.
  Oh, silence my lips with a kiss,
My lips that are weary of song!

Shelter my soul, O my Love!
  My soul is bent low with the pain
And the burden of love, like the grace
  Of a flower that is smitten with rain;
Oh, shelter my soul from thy face!

Sarojini Naidu

THE MAN WITH A HAMMER

My Dear was a mason
  And I was his stone.
And quick did he fashion
  A house of his own.

As fish in the waters,
  As birds in a tree,
So natural and blithe lives
  His spirit in me.

Anna Wickham

THE GREAT MAN

I CANNOT always feel his greatness.
Sometimes he walks beside me, step by step,
And paces slowly in the ways —
The simple, wingless ways
That my thoughts tread. He gossips with me
       then,
And finds it good;
Not as an eagle might, his great wings folded,
      be content
To walk a little, knowing it his choice,
But as a simple man,
My friend.
And I forget.

Then suddenly a call floats down
From the clear airy spaces,
The great keen, lonely heights of being.
And he who was my comrade hears the call
And rises from my side, and soars,
Deep-chanting, to the heights.

37

The Answering Voice

Then I remember.
And my upward gaze goes with him, and I see
Far off against the sky
The glint of golden sunlight on his wings.

Eunice Tietjens

I KNOW

Oh! I know why the alder trees
   Lean over the reflecting stream;
And I know what the wandering bees
   Heard in the woods of dream.

I know how the uneasy tide
   Answers the signal of the moon,
And why the morning-glories hide
   Their eyes in the forenoon.

And I know all the wild delight
   That quivers in the sea-bird's wings,
For in one little hour last night
   Love told me all these things.

Elsa Barker

REST

As a little child I come
To be gathered to your breast
So tired that my lips are dumb,
So sad that my warm heart is numb:
 Belovèd, let me rest.

Oh, how all the noises die,
All the cruel voices cease,
I can sleep when you are by,
And I am too faint to cry:
 Here at last is peace.

Hold me, nurse me, love me . . . so . . .
Almost I could learn to weep!
Hush, I feel my spirit grow . . .
When you tire . . . let me go . . .
 I shall be . . . asleep.

Irene Rutherford McLeod

"IF THOU MUST LOVE ME, LET IT BE FOR NOUGHT"

If thou must love me, let it be for nought
Except for love's sake only. Do not say,
"I love her for her smile, her look, her way
Of speaking gently, for a trick of thought
That falls in well with mine, and certes brought
A sense of pleasant ease on such a day";
For these things in themselves, belovèd, may
Be changed, or change for thee : and love so wrought
May be unwrought so. Neither love me for
Thine own dear pity's wiping my cheeks dry :
A creature might forget to weep, who bore
Thy comfort long, and lose thy love thereby.
But love me for love's sake, that evermore
Thou mayst love on through love's eternity.

Elizabeth Barrett Browning

THE TIRED WOMAN

O MY Lover, blind me,
Take your cords and bind me,
Then drive me through a silent land,
With the compelling of your open hand!

There is too much of sound, too much for sight,
In thunderous lightnings of this night,
There is too much of freedom for my feet,
Bruised by the stones of this disordered street.

I know that there is sweetest rest for me,
In silent fields, and in captivity.
O Lover! drive me through a stilly land,
With the compelling of your open hand.

Anna Wickham

"HOW DO I LOVE THEE?"

How do I love thee? Let me count the ways.
I love thee to the depth and breadth and height
My soul can reach, when feeling out of sight
For the ends of being and ideal grace.
I love thee to the level of every day's
Most quiet need, by sun and candle-light.
I love thee freely, as men strive for right.
I love thee purely, as they turn from praise.
I love thee with the passion put to use
In my old griefs, and with my childhood's faith.
I love thee with a love I seemed to lose
With my lost saints. I love thee with the breath,
Smiles, tears, of all my life; and, if God choose,
I shall but love thee better after death.

Elizabeth Barrett Browning

THE TAXI

When I go away from you
The world beats dead
Like a slackened drum.
I call out for you against the jutted stars
And shout into the ridges of the wind.
Streets coming fast,
One after the other,
Wedge you away from me,
And the lamps of the city prick my eyes
So that I can no longer see your face.
Why should I leave you,
To wound myself upon the sharp edges of the night?

Amy Lowell

"YOU SAY THERE IS NO LOVE"

You say there is no love, my love,
   Unless it lasts for aye!
Oh, folly, there are interludes
   Better than the play.

You say lest it endure, sweet love,
   It is not love for aye?
Oh, blind! Eternity can be
   All in one little day.

Grace Fallow Norton

45

DEBTS

My debt to you, Belovèd,
  Is one I cannot pay
In any coin of any realm
  On any reckoning day;

For where is he shall figure
  The debt, when all is said,
To one who makes you dream again
  When all the dreams were dead?

Or where is the appraiser
  Who shall the claim compute
Of one who makes you sing again
  When all the songs were mute?

Jessie B. Rittenhouse

A WOMAN'S QUESTION

BEFORE I trust my fate to thee,
   Or place my hand in thine,
Before I let thy future give
   Color and form to mine, —
Before I peril all for thee, question thy soul
      to-night, for me.

I break all slighter bonds, nor feel
   One shadow of regret :
Is there one link within the past
   That holds thy spirit yet ?
Or is thy faith as clear and free as that which
      I can pledge to thee ? . . .

Is there within thy heart a need
   That mine cannot fulfill ?
One chord that any other hand
   Could better wake or still ?
Speak now, lest at some future day, my whole
      life wither and decay. . . .

THE ANSWERING VOICE

Couldst thou withdraw thy hand one day,
    And answer to my claim
That fate, and that to-day's mistake,
    Not thou, had been to blame?
Some soothe their conscience thus; but thou — oh,
    surely thou wilt warn me now!

Adelaide Anne Procter

COMRADES

You need not say one word to me, as up the hill
  we go
(Night-time, white-time, all in the whispering
   snow);
You need not say one word to me, although the
  whispering trees
Seem strange and old as pagan priests in swaying
  mysteries.

You need not think one thought of me, as up the
  trail we go
(Hill-trail, still-trail, all in the hiding snow);
You need not think one thought of me, although a
  hare runs by,
And off behind the tumbled cairn we hear a red fox
  cry.

Oh, good and rare it is to feel, as through the
  night we go
(Wild-wise, child-wise, all in the secret snow),

The Answering Voice

That we are free of heart and foot as hare and fox
    are free,
And yet that I am glad of you, and you are glad
    of me!

Fannie Stearns Davis

IN DEEP PLACES

I LOVE thee, dear, and knowing mine own heart
With every beat I give God thanks for this;
I love thee only for the self thou art;
No wild embrace, no wisdom-shaking kiss,
No passionate pleading of a heart laid bare,
No urgent cry of love's extremity —
Strong traps to take the spirit unaware —
Not one of these I ever had of thee.
Neither of passion nor of pity wrought
Is this, the love to which at last I yield,
But shapen in the stillness of my thought
And by a birth of agony revealed.
Here is a thing to live while we do live
Which honors thee to take and me to give.

Amelia Josephine Burr

THAT DAY YOU CAME

Such special sweetness was about
　　That day God sent you here,
I knew the lavender was out,
　　And it was mid of year.

Their common way the great winds blew,
　　The ships sailed out to sea;
Yet ere that day was spent I knew
　　Mine own had come to me.

As after song some snatch of tune
　　Lurks still in grass or bough,
So, somewhat of the end o' June
　　Lurks in each weather now.

The young year sets the buds astir,
　　The old year strips the trees;
But ever in my lavender
　　I hear the brawling bees.

Lizette Woodworth Reese

PARTING

My life closed twice before its close;
    It yet remains to see
If Immortality unveil
    A third event to me.

So huge, so hopeless to conceive,
    As these that twice befell;
Parting is all we know of heaven,
    And all we need of hell.

Emily Dickinson

AN OLD SONG

And if I came not again
After certain days;
If no morning sun or rain
Met me on their ways;

If the meadows knew no more
How my feet go free,
And the folded hills forbore
Any speech of me;

If you did not find me here,
At the door at night,
And the cold hearth kept no cheer,
And the panes no light; —

Oh, if I came not again,
Would you miss me much?
Would your fingers once be fain
Of my wandering touch?

An Old Song

Would you dream me at your side
In the waking wood,
Where the old spring hungers hide
In blue solitude?

Would you wonder where I passed,
Into joy or pain?
Oh, to know you cared, at last,
Came I not again!

Fannie Stearns Davis

"I WILL NOT GIVE THEE ALL MY HEART"

I WILL not give thee all my heart
For that I need a place apart
To dream my dreams in, and I know
Few sheltered ways for dreams to go:
But when I shut the door upon
Some secret wonder — still, withdrawn —
Why dost thou love me even more,
And hold me closer than before?

When I of Love demand the least,
Thou biddest him to fire and feast:
When I am hungry and would eat,
There is no bread, though crusts were sweet.
If I with manna may be fed,
Shall I go all uncomforted?
Nay! Howsoever dear thou art,
I will not give thee all my heart.

Grace Hazard Conkling

GIFTS

You ask me what — since we must part —
  You shall bring back to me.
Bring back a pure and faithful heart
  As true as mine to thee.

You talk of gems from foreign lands,
  Of treasure, spoil, and prize.
Ah love! I shall not search your hands
  But look into your eyes.

Juliana Horatia Ewing

MENACE

I CAME into your room and spoke.
   Sudden I knew you were not there.
The easy, common sentence broke
   Against the unanswering air.

My heart shook like a frightened bird,
   And to my ear the terror said,
Where nothing spoke and nothing stirred, —
   Dear God, if he were dead!

I heard your footstep in the house,
   Your voice brought comfort to my fear.
But, fluttering like a frightened mouse,
   My heart beat at my ear.

The room wore its familiar face;
   On the warm hearth spirted the flame.
Yet — menace of an empty place —
   Lord, if he never came!

Katharine Tynan

LOVE SONG

I LOVE my life, but not too well
   To give it to thee like a flower,
So it may pleasure thee to dwell
   Deep in its perfume but an hour.
I love my life, but not too well.

I love my life, but not too well
   To sing it note by note away,
So to thy soul the song may tell
   The beauty of the desolate day.
I love my life, but not too well.

I love my life, but not too well
   To cast it like a cloak on thine,
Against the storms that sound and swell
   Between thy lonely heart and mine.
I love my life, but not too well.

Harriet Monroe

POSSESSION

Walk into the world,
Go into the places of trade;
Go into the smiling country —
But go, clad, wrapped closely always,
Shielded and sustained,
In the visible flame of my love.

Let it blaze about you —
A glowing armor for all to see;
Flashing around your head —
A tender and valiant halo.

I think there will be many to wonder
And many to stand in awe and envy —
But surely no one will come too close to you.
No one will dare to claim you, —
Hand or heart, —
As you pass in your shining and terrible garment.

Jean Starr Untermeyer

"YET FOR ONE ROUNDED MOMENT"

YET for one rounded moment I will be
No more to you than what my lips may give,
And in the circle of your kisses live
As in some island of a storm-blown sea,
Where the cold surges of infinity
Upon the outward reefs unheeded grieve,
And the loud murmur of our blood shall weave
Primeval silences round you and me.

If in that moment we are all we are,
We live enough. Let this for all requite.
Do I not know, some wingèd things from far
Are borne along illimitable night
To dance their lives out in a single flight
Between the moonrise and the setting star?

Edith Wharton

INSUFFICIENCY

I

THERE is no one beside thee, and no one above thee;
  Thou standest alone, as the nightingale sings!
  And my words that would praise thee are impotent things,
For none can express thee, though all should approve thee.
  I love thee so, dear, that I only can love thee.

II

Say, what can I do for thee? Weary thee, grieve thee?
  Lean on thy shoulder, new burdens to add?
  Weep my tears over thee, making thee sad?
Oh, hold me not, love me not! let me retrieve thee.
  I love thee so, dear, that I only can leave thee.
                                        Elizabeth Barrett Browning

"I MUST NOT YIELD"

I MUST not yield . . . but if he would not sing!
  My stilling hands upon my breast can feel
Its answer tremble like a muted string.
  Below the vaulted window where I kneel

He sings, he sings, to stars and listening skies.
  A white and haunted place my garden seems.—
I see the pleading beauty of his eyes
  As faces glimmer in a pool of dreams.

So wooing wind might sweep a harp awake.
  (Oh, muting fingers on each quivering string!)
I must not yield . . . I think my heart will break.
  Mother of Heaven, if he would not sing!
                                Nora May French

"GO FROM ME"

Go from me. Yet I feel that I shall stand
Henceforward in thy shadow. Nevermore
Alone upon the threshold of my door
Of individual life, I shall command
The uses of my soul, nor lift my hand
Serenely in the sunshine as before,
Without the sense of that which I forbore, —
Thy touch upon the palm. The widest land
Doom takes to part us leaves thy heart in mine
With pulses that beat double. What I do
And what I dream include thee, as the wine
Must taste of its own grapes. And, when I sue
God for myself, he hears that name of thine,
And sees within my eyes the tears of two.

Elizabeth Barrett Browning

RENOUNCEMENT

I must not think of thee; and, tired yet strong,
  I shun the thought that lurks in all delight —
  The thought of thee — and in the blue Heaven's
      height,
And in the sweetest passage of a song.

Oh, just beyond the fairest thoughts that throng
  This breast, the thought of thee waits, hidden
     yet bright;
  But it must never, never come in sight;
I must stop short of thee the whole day long.

But when sleep comes to close each difficult day,
  When night gives pause to the long watch I keep,
    And all my bonds I needs must loose apart,

Must doff my will as raiment laid away, —
  With the first dream that comes with the first sleep
    I run, I run, I am gathered to thy heart.
                Alice Meynell

A FAREWELL

Good-bye! — no, do not grieve that it is over,
   The perfect hour;
That the winged joy, sweet honey-loving rover,
   Flits from the flower.

Grieve not — it is the law. Love will be flying —
   Yes, love and all.
Glad was the living — blessed be the dying.
   Let the leaves fall.

Harriet Monroe

LOVE'S CHANGE

I WENT to dig a grave for Love,
　　But the earth was so stiff and cold
That, though I strove through the bitter night,
　　I could not break the mould.

And I said: "Must he lie in my house in state,
　　And stay in his wonted place?
Must I have him with me another day,
　　With that awful change in his face?"

Anne Reeve Aldrich

WHEN PLAINTIVELY AND NEAR THE CRICKET SINGS

Now evening comes. Now stirs my discontent . . .
  Oh, ache of smallest, unforgotten things!
How sharp you are when day and dark are blent
  When beetles hurry by with vibrant wings,
  And plaintively and near the cricket sings.

The sighing garden calls me from the door;
  Above the hills a little crescent swings —
Above the path where you will come no more
  When beetles hurry by on vibrant wings,
  And plaintively and near the cricket sings.

Nora May French

"COME BACK TO ME"

Come back to me, who wait and watch for you : —
　　Or come not yet, for it is over then,
　　And long it is before you come again,
So far between my pleasures are and few.
While, when you come not, what I do I do
　　Thinking, " Now when he comes," my sweetest
　　　　" when " :
　　For one man is my world of all the men
This wide world holds; O love, my world is you.
Howbeit, to meet you grows almost a pang
　　Because the pang of parting comes so soon;
　　My hope hangs waning, waxing, like a moon
　　Between the heavenly days on which we meet :
Ah me, but where are now the songs I sang
　　When life was sweet because you called them
　　　　sweet?

Christina Rossetti

ASHES OF LIFE

Love has gone and left me and the days are all
    alike;
  Eat I must, and sleep I will, — and would that
    night were here!
But ah! — to lie awake and hear the slow hours
    strike!
  Would that it were day again! — with twilight
    near!

Love has gone and left me and I don't know what
    to do;
  This or that or what you will is all the same to
    me;
But all the things that I begin I leave before I 'm
    through, —
  There 's little use in anything as far as I can
    see.

Love has gone and left me, and the neighbors knock
    and borrow,

ASHES OF LIFE

And life goes on forever like the gnawing of a
    mouse. —
And to-morrow and to-morrow and to-morrow
    and to-morrow
There's this little street and this little house.

Edna St. Vincent Millay

THE CYNIC

I say it to comfort me over and over,
  Having a querulous heart to beguile,
Never had woman a tenderer lover —
  For a little while.

Oh, there never were eyes more eager to read her
  In her saddest mood or her moments gay,
Oh, there never were hands more strong to lead
      her —
  For a little way.

There never were loftier promises given
  Of love that should guard her the ages through,
As great, enduring and steadfast as Heaven —
  For a week or two.

Well, end as it does, I have had it, known it,
  For this shall I turn me to weep or pray?
Nay, rather I laugh that I thought to own it
  For more than a day.

Theodosia Garrison

SEA SONG

Against the planks of the cabin side
  (So slight a thing between them and me),
The great waves thundered and throbbed and
        sighed,
  The great green waves of the Indian Sea!

Your face was white as the foam is white,
  Your hair was curled as the waves are curled,
I would we had steamed and reached that night
  The sea's last edge, the end of the world.

The wind blew in through the open port,
  So freshly joyous and salt and free,
Your hair it lifted, your lips it sought,
  And then swept back to the open sea.

The engines throbbed with their constant beat;
  Your heart was nearer, and all I heard;
Your lips were salt, but I found them sweet,
  While, acquiescent, you spoke no word.

The Answering Voice

So straight you lay in your narrow berth,
  Rocked by the waves; and you seemed to be
Essence of all that is sweet on earth,
  Of all that is sad and strange at sea.

And you were white as the foam is white,
  Your hair was curled as the waves are curled.
Ah! had we but sailed and reached that night,
  The sea's last edge, the end of the world!

Laurence Hope

RISPETTO

WHAT good is there, ah me, what good in Love?
   Since, even if you love me, we must part;
And since for either, an' you cared enough,
   There's but division and a broken heart?

And yet, God knows, to hear you say: My Dear!
I would lie down and stretch me on the bier.
And yet would I, to hear you say: My Own!
With mine own hands drag down the burial stone.

A. Mary F. Robinson

RISPETTO

LET us forget we loved each other much,
  Let us forget we ever have to part,
Let us forget that any look or touch
  Once let in either to the other's heart.

Only we 'll sit upon the daisied grass
And hear the larks and see the swallows pass;
Only we 'll live awhile, as children play,
Without to-morrow, without yesterday.

A. Mary F. Robinson

RISPETTO

III

Ah, Love, I cannot die, I cannot go
   Down in the dark and leave you all alone,
Ah, hold me fast, safe in the warmth I know,
   And never shut me underneath a stone.

Dead in the grave! And I can never hear
If you are ill, or if you miss me, dear,
Dead, oh, my God! and you may need me yet,
While I shall sleep, while I — while I — forget!

A. Mary F. Robinson

"MANY IN AFTERTIMES WILL SAY"

MANY in aftertimes will say of you,
  "He loved her" — while of me what will they
    say?
  Not that I loved you more than just in play,
For fashion's sake as idle women do.
Even let them prate; who know not what we knew
  Of love and parting in exceeding pain,
  Of parting hopeless here to meet again,
Hopeless on earth, and heaven is out of view.
But by my heart of love laid bare to you,
  My love that you can make not void nor vain,
Love that foregoes you but to claim anew
Beyond this passage of the gate of death,
  I charge you at the Judgment make it plain
My love of you was life and not a breath.

Christina Rossetti

"WHEN WE SHALL BE DUST"

WHEN we shall be dust in the churchyard —
   In twenty years — in fifty years —
Who will remember you kissed me once,
   Who will be grieved for our tears?

The locust tree will have grown taller,
   The old walks will be covered with grass,
And past our quiet graves go straying
   A youth with his arm round his lass.

And the bee that shall suck your grave flowers —
   Anemone, stock, columbine,
May pause in his swift homing journey
   To taste of the honey from mine.

Muna Lee

I AM THE WIND

I AM the wind that wavers,
    You are the certain land;
I am the shadow that passes
    Over the sand.

I am the leaf that quivers,
    You — the unshaken tree;
You are the stars that are steadfast,
    I am the sea.

You are the light eternal,
    Like a torch I shall die. . . .
You are the surge of deep music.
    I — but a cry!

Zoë Akins

SERVICE

If I could only serve him,
  How sweet this life would be.
Last night I dreamed my darling,
  Alive, returned to me.

I brought him from the cupboard
  The things he liked to eat, —
The little piece of honey,
  The rye bread and the meat.

I sang the song he asked for
  The night he went away.
How was it, when I loved him,
  I could have said him nay!

I took the time to please him,
  With a hand upon his brow.
Amid the awful leisure
  There was no hurry now.

THE ANSWERING VOICE

How strange I once denied him
    What took so little while.
A kiss would seem so simple,
    So slight a thing a smile.

With pleased sweet looks of wonder
    He took what I could give, —
Such words as we deny them
    Only because they live.

The pale light of the morning
    Shone in upon the wall.
Come back to me, my darling,
    And I will give you all.

Anna Hempstead Branch

PARTING

Dear Love, it was so hard to say
      Good-bye to-day!
You turned to go, yet going turned to stay!
Till suddenly at last you went away.

Then all at last I found my love unsaid,
      And bowed my head;
And went in tears up to my lonely bed —
Oh, would it be like this if you were dead?
               Alice Freeman Palmer

FRIENDSHIP AFTER LOVE

AFTER the fierce midsummer all ablaze
   Has burned itself to ashes, and expires
   In the intensity of its own fires,
There come the mellow, mild, St. Martin days
Crowned with the calm of peace, but sad with haze;
   So after Love has led us, till he tires
   Of his own throes, and torments, and desires
Comes large-eyed friendship; with a restful gaze,
He beckons us to follow, and across
   Cool, verdant vales we wander free from care —
   Is it a touch of frost lies in the air?
Why are we haunted with a sense of loss?
We do not wish the pain back, or the heat;
And yet, and yet, these days are incomplete.

Ella Wheeler Wilcox

THE MESSAGE

"Oh, have you not a message, you who come over
    the sea ?
Have you not a message or word at all for me?"

"I have sailed, sailed, sailed where the seas are
    green and blue,
I've silver, gold and merchandise — but never a
    word for you."

"But did you see my love by any way you came ?
For if you saw my love, he must have spoke my
    name."

"Oh, yes, I saw your love — oh, yes, and he was gay
Riding in his coach-and-six all on his birthday."

"But when you spoke of me, of me — oh! what
    was it he said ? "
"Oh, he never said a word at all, but turned away
    his head."

Margaret Sackville

THE OTHER

I AM the Other — I who come
    To heal the wound she gave,
The wound that struck your fond words dumb
    And left your world a grave.

What though you loved her — I love you,
    And so the most is said,
Here is my yearning heart, still true
    To yours her frailty bled.

(But oh! the bitter grief that I
    Kept hushed, the wild despair,
When your dear eyes had passed me by
    To find her face so fair.)

Now she hath gone her cruel way,
    And I am come again,
To seek among the husks to-day,
    For one sweet golden grain.

THE OTHER

Because in me Love's strength is great,
    Too great for pride, or sin,
I knock upon your heart's barred gate,
    And pray you let me in.

Ethna Carbery

THE RAINBOW

Whose doorway was it, in the sordid street,
    That gave us shelter from the sudden rain, —
Two vagrant sparrows on a dripping branch,
    Waiting a moment to spread wing again?

The beggar children danced through pavement pools
    Barefoot and joyous, splashing at their will;
The rain washed green that dusty sycamore
    And straws swirled wildly down the gutter's rill.

Fast-breathing from the run, our hands still clasped,
    We leaned out laughing, shaking free our hair
Of dewy drops, while still the clouds poured down
    A freshness that made heavenly the air.

Then we both saw, above the sodden world,
    The Rainbow like a miracle appear,
And you said, whispering, "Oh, kiss me once
    Before it fades!" — "Kiss me then quickly,
        Dear!"

The Rainbow

One warm sweet touch of lips — then forth we
　　went
　Oblivious of all the rain and wet.
To-day I saw a rainbow after rain. . . .
　My heart remembered then — does yours forget?

Vine Colby

LOVE CAME BACK AT FALL O' DEW

Love came back at fall o' dew,
  Playing his old part;
But I had a word or two
That would break his heart.

" He who comes at candle-light,
  That should come before,
Must betake him to the night
From a barrèd door."

This the word that made us part
In the fall o' dew;
This the word that brake his heart —
Yet it brake mine, too.

Lizette Woodworth Reese

FROM A CAR-WINDOW

PINES, and a blur of lithe young grasses;
   Gold in a pool, from the western glow;
Spread of wings where the last thrush passes —
   And thoughts of you as the sun dips low.

Quiet lane, and an irised meadow . . .
   (*How many summers have died since then?*) . . .
I wish you knew how the deepening shadow
   Lies on the blue and green again!

Dusk, and the curve of field and hollow
   Etched in gray when a star appears:
Sunset, . . . twilight, . . . and dark to follow, . . .
   And thoughts of you through a mist of tears.
                    Ruth Guthrie Harding

THE SILLER CROWN

" AND ye sall walk in silk attire,
    And siller hae to spare,
Gin ye 'll consent to be his bride,
    Nor think o' Donald mair."

O, wha wad buy a silken gown
    Wi' a puir broken heart?
Or what 's to me a siller crown
    Gin frae my love I part?

The mind whose meanest wish is pure
    Far dearest is to me,
And ere I 'm forced to break my faith,
    I 'll lay me down and dee.

For I hae vowed a virgin's vow
    My lover's faith to share,
An' he has gi'en to me his heart,
    An' what can man do mair?

THE SILLER CROWN

His mind and manners won my heart,
  He gratefu' took the gift,
An' did I wish to seek it back
  It wad be waur than theft.

The langest life can ne'er repay
  The love he bears to me,
And ere I 'm forced to break my faith,
  I 'll lay me down an' dee.

Susanna Blamire

"CUTTIN' RUSHES"

OH, maybe it was yesterday, or fifty years ago!
  Meself was risin' early on a day for cuttin'
        rushes.
Walkin' up the Brabla' burn, still the sun was low,
  Now I 'd hear the burn run an' then I 'd hear
        the thrushes.
Young, still young! — and drenchin' wet the grass,
  Wet the golden honeysuckle hangin' sweetly
        down;
Here, lad, here! will ye follow where I pass,
  An' find me cuttin' rushes on the mountain.

Then was it only yesterday, or fifty years or so?
  Rippin' round the bog pools high among the
        heather,
The hook it made me hand sore, I had to leave
        it go,
  'T was he that cut the rushes then for me to
        bind together.
Come, dear, come! — an' back along the burn

94

"CUTTIN' RUSHES"

See the darlin' honeysuckle hangin' like a crown.
Quick, one kiss, — sure, there 's some one at the
turn !
    " Oh, we 're afther cuttin' rushes on the moun-
    tain."

Yesterday, yesterday, or fifty years ago. . . .
    I waken out o' dreams when I hear the sum-
    mer thrushes.
Oh, that 's the Brabla' burn, I can hear it sing an'
flow,
    For all that 's fair I 'd sooner see a bunch o'
    green rushes.
Run, burn, run! can ye mind when we were
young ?
    The honeysuckle hangs above, the pool is dark
    an' brown :
Sing, burn, sing! can ye mind the song ye sung
    The day we cut the rushes on the mountain ?

Moira O'Neill

TO A LATE COMER

Why didst thou come into my life so late?
  If it were morning I could welcome thee
  With glad all-hails, and bid each hour to be
The willing servitor of thine estate,
Lading thy brave ships with Time's richest freight;
  If it were noonday I might hope to see
  On some fair height thy banners floating free,
And hear the acclaiming voices call thee great!
But it is nightfall and the stars are out;
  Far in the west the crescent moon hangs low,
    And near at hand the lurking shadows wait;
Darkness and silence gather round about,
  Lethe's black stream is near its overflow, —
    Ah, friend, dear friend, why didst thou come
      so late?

Julia C. R. Dorr

CARNATIONS

Carnations and my first love! And he was seven-
   teen,
And I was only twelve years — a stately gulf be-
   tween!
I broke them on the morning the school-dance was
   to be,
To pin among my ribbons in hopes that he might
   see. . . .
And all the girls stood breathless to watch as he
   came through
With curly crest and grand air that swept the heart
   from you!
And why he paused at my side is more than I can
   know —
Shyest of the small girls who all adored him
   so —
I said it with my prayer-times: I walked with
   head held high:
" *Carnations are your flower!* " he said as he
   strode by.

The Answering Voice

Carnations and my first love! The years are
    passed a score,
And I recall his first name, and scarce an eyelash
    more. . . .
And those were all the love-words that either of
    us said —
Perhaps he may be married — perhaps he may be
    dead.
And yet, . . . to smell carnations, their spicy,
    heavy sweet,
Perfuming all some sick-room, or passing on the
    street,
Then . . . still the school-lamps flicker, and still
    the Lancers play,
And still the girls hold breathless to watch him go
    his way,
And still my child-heart quivers with that first
    ecstasy —
"Carnations are your flower!" my first love says
    to me!

                      Margaret Widdemer

A REMINISCENCE

It is so long gone by, and yet
    How clearly now I see it all!
The glimmer of your cigarette,
    The little chamber, narrow and tall.

Perseus; your picture in its frame;
    (How near they seem and yet how far!)
The blaze of kindled logs; the flame
    Of tulips in a mighty jar.

Florence and spring-time: surely each
    Glad things unto the spirit saith.
Why did you lead me in your speech
    To these dark mysteries of death?

Amy Levy

DIRGE

NEVER the nightingale;
   Oh, my dear,
Never again the lark,
   Thou wilt hear.
Though dusk and the morning still
Tap at thy window-sill,
Though ever love call and call,
Thou wilt not hear at all,
   My dear, my dear.

Adelaide Crapsey

"TO–DAY I WENT AMONG THE MOUNTAIN FOLK"

To-day I went among the mountain folk
To hear the gentle talk most dear to me.
I saw slow tears, and tenderness that woke
From sternest bed to light a lamp for thee.
And "Is it true?" hope asked and asked again,
And "It is true," was all that I could say,
And pride rose over love to hide gray pain
As eyes tears might ungrace were turned away.
So much they loved thee I was half decoyed
By human warmth to feel thee near, but when
I put my hand out all the earth was void,
And vanished even these near-weeping men.
Thus each new time I find that thou art gone,
Anew do I survive the world, alone.

Olive Tilford Dargan

AN APRIL GHOST

ALL the ghosts I ever knew,
   White, and thinly calling,
Come into the house with you,
   When the dew is falling.

All of youth that ever died,
   In the Spring-time weather,
In the windy April tide,
   Climb the dusk together.

For a moment, lad and maid
   Stand up there all lonely;
In a moment fade and fade—
   You are left, you only.

              Lizette Woodworth Reese

THE DEEP-SEA PEARL

THE love of my life came not
    As love unto others is cast;
For mine was a secret wound —
    But the wound grew a pearl, at last.

The divers may come and go,
    The tides, they arise and fall;
The pearl in its shell lies sealed,
    And the Deep Sea covers all.

Edith M. Thomas

AULD ROBIN GRAY

WHEN the sheep are in the fauld, when the kye 's
come hame,
And a' the weary warld to rest are gane,
The waes o' my heart fa' in showers frae my ee,
Unkent by my gudeman, wha sleeps sound by
me.

Young Jamie lo'ed me weel, and sought me for his
bride,
But saving ae crown-piecè he had naething beside;
To make the crown a pound my Jamie gaed to
sea,
And the crown and the pound — they were baith
for me.

He hadna been gane a twelvemonth and a day,
When my father brake his arm and the cow was
stown away;
My mither she fell sick — my Jamie was at sea,
And auld Robin Gray came a-courting me.

Auld Robin Gray

My father couldna wark — my mither couldna
      spin —
I toiled day and night, but their bread I couldna win;
Auld Rob maintained them baith, and, wi' tears in
      his ee,
Said: "Jeanie, O for their sakes, will ye no marry
      me?"

My heart it said na, and I looked for Jamie back,
But hard blew the winds, and his ship was a wrack;
His ship was a wrack — why didna Jamie dee?
Or why am I spared to cry wae is me?

My father urged me sair — my mither didna speak,
But she looked in my face till my heart was like
      to break;
They gied him my hand — my heart was in the sea —
And so Robin Gray he was gudeman to me.

I hadna been his wife a week but only four,
When, mournfu' as I sat on the stane at my door,
I saw my Jamie's ghaist, for I couldna think it he,
Till he said: "I'm come hame, love, to marry
      thee!"

The Answering Voice

Oh, sair, sair did we greet, and mickle say of a',
I gied him ae kiss, and bade him gang awa' —
I wish that I were dead, but I'm na like to dee,
For, though my heart is broken, I'm but young,
      wae is me!

I gang like a ghaist, and I carena much to spin,
I darena think o' Jamie, for that wad be a sin,
But I'll do my best a gude wife to be,
For, oh! Robin Gray, he is kind to me.

Anne Barnard

FINIS

Even for you I shall not weep
   When I at last, at last am dead,
Nor turn and sorrow in my sleep
   Though you should linger overhead.

Even of you I shall not dream
   Beneath the waving graveyard grass;
One with the soul of wind and stream
   I shall not heed you if you pass.

Even for you I would not wake,
   Too bitter were the tears I knew,
Too dark the road I needs must take —
   The road that winds away from you.
Rosamund Marriott Watson

"GRANDMITHER, THINK NOT I FORGET"

GRANDMITHER, think not I forget, when I come
    back to town,
An' wander the old ways again an' tread them up
    an' down.
I never smell the clover bloom, nor see the swal-
    lows pass,
Without I mind how good ye were unto a little lass.
I never hear the winter rain a-pelting all night
    through,
Without I think and mind me of how cold it falls
    on you.
And if I come not often to your bed beneath the
    thyme,
Mayhap 't is that I 'd change wi' ye, and gie my
    bed for thine,
        Would like to sleep in thine.

I never hear the summer winds among the roses blow,
Without I wonder why it was ye loved the lassie so.

"GRANDMITHER, THINK NOT I FORGET"

Ye gave me cakes and lollipops and pretty toys a
        score, —
I never thought I should come back and ask ye
        now for more.
Grandmither, gie me your still, white hands, that
        lie upon your breast,
For mine do beat the dark all night and never find
        me rest;
They grope among the shadows an' they beat the
        cold black air,
They go seekin' in the darkness, an' they never find
        him there,
        An' they never find him there.

Grandmither, gie me your sightless eyes, that I
        may never see
His own a-burnin' full o' love that must not shine
        for me.
Grandmither, gie me your peaceful lips, white as
        the kirkyard snow,
For mine be red wi' burnin' thirst an' he must
        never know.
Grandmither, gie me your clay-stopped ears, that
        I may never hear

The Answering Voice

My lad a-singin' in the night when I am sick wi' fear;
A-singin' when the moonlight over a' the land is
    white —
Oh God! I'll up an' go to him a-singin' in the
    night,
       A-callin' in the night.

Grandmither, give me your clay-cold heart that
    has forgot to ache,
For mine be fire within my breast and yet it can-
    not break.
It beats an' throbs forever for the things that must
    not be, —
An' can ye not let me creep in an' rest awhile by ye?
A little lass afeared o' dark slept by ye years
    agone —
Ah, she has found what night can hold 'twixt sun-
    set an' the dawn!
So when I plant the rose an' rue above your grave
    for ye,
Ye'll know it's under rue an' rose that I would
    like to be,
       That I would like to be.

Willa Sibert Cather

THE PASSER–BY

Step lightly across the floor,
And somewhat more tender be.

There were many that passed my door,
Many that sought after me.
I gave them the passing word —
Ah, why did I give thee more?
I gave thee what could not be heard,
What had not been given before;
The beat of my heart I gave. . . .
And I give thee this flower on my grave.

My face in the flower thou mayst see.
Step lightly across the floor.

Edith M. Thomas

111

"WHEN I AM DEAD"

WHEN I am dead, my dearest,
  Sing no sad songs for me;
Plant thou no roses at my head,
  Nor shady cypress tree:
Be the green grass above me
  With showers and dewdrops wet:
And if thou wilt, remember,
  And if thou wilt, forget.

I shall not see the shadows,
  I shall not feel the rain;
I shall not hear the nightingale
  Sing on as if in pain:
And dreaming through the twilight
  That doth not rise nor set,
Haply I may remember,
  And haply may forget.

Christina Rossetti

REQUIESCAT

BURY me deep when I am dead,
Far from the woods where sweet birds sing;
Lap me in sullen stone and lead,
Lest my poor dust should feel the Spring.

Never a flower be near me set,
Nor starry cup nor slender stem,
Anemone nor violet,
Lest my poor dust remember them.

And you — wherever you may fare —
Dearer than birds, or flowers, or dew —
Never, ah me, pass never there,
Lest my poor dust should dream of you.

Rosamund Marriott Watson

"DOUGLAS, DOUGLAS, TENDER AND TRUE"

Could ye come back to me, Douglas, Douglas,
In the old likeness that I knew,
I would be so faithful, so loving, Douglas,
Douglas, Douglas, tender and true.

Never a scornful word should grieve ye,
I'd smile on ye sweet as the angels do; —
Sweet as your smile on me shone ever,
Douglas, Douglas, tender and true.

Oh, to call back the days that are not!
My eyes were blinded, your words were few;
Do you know the truth now up in heaven,
Douglas, Douglas, tender and true?

I never was worthy of you, Douglas;
Not half worthy the like of you:
Now all men beside seem to me like shadows —
I love you, Douglas, tender and true.

114

DOUGLAS, DOUGLAS, TENDER AND TRUE

Stretch out your hand to me, Douglas, Douglas,
Drop forgiveness from heaven like dew;
As I lay my heart on your dead heart, Douglas,
Douglas, Douglas, tender and true.

Dinah Mulock Craik

UNWEDDED

ALONG her tranquil way she went,
  The slow, sad course of changeless years,
While in her burned her youth unspent,
  Dulled sometimes by her gentle tears.

In richer lives she saw the strange,
  Sweet urgency of wedded days;
In dreams she watched her pale light change,
  Into the steadfast altar blaze.

And, waking, sadly bowed above
  Her slender vestal flame and wept;
Ah, better were the house of love,
  By blighting fire and tempest swept.

Ada Foster Murray

UNFULFILLED

I READ the pain and pathos of your eyes,
  The aftermath of anguish in your smile,
  And yet I can but envy you the while!
Your heart has bled, an ardent sacrifice
To Love's fulfillment. You have paid the price
  Of keen, fierce living; nor can aught defile
  The joys that once have been — they still beguile
The tear-swept memory that Time defies.

My soul's adventure, pallid, incomplete,
  Has lingered in the twilight, for my heart
    Has dwelt aloof in some dim atmosphere
Betwixt the Earth and Heaven. My alien feet
  Have known nor Pain nor its great counterpart.
    I, who have never loved, may shed no tear.
                          Corinne Roosevelt Robinson

117

A LYNMOUTH WIDOW

HE was straight and strong, and his eyes were blue
As the summer meeting of sky and sea,
And the ruddy cliffs had a colder hue
Than flushed his cheek when he married me.

We passed the porch where the swallows breed,
We left the little brown church behind,
And I leaned on his arm, though I had no need,
Only to feel him so strong and kind.

One thing I never can quite forget;
It grips my throat when I try to pray —
The keen salt smell of a drying net
That hung on the churchyard wall that day.

He would have taken a long, long grave —
A long, long grave, for he stood so tall . . .
Oh, God! the crash of a breaking wave,
And the smell of the nets on the churchyard wall!

Amelia Josephine Burr

118

"LESS THAN THE DUST"

Less than the dust, beneath thy Chariot wheel,
Less than the rust, that never stained thy Sword,
Less than the trust thou hast in me, O Lord,
                    Even less than these!

Less than the weed, that grows beside thy door,
Less than the speed of hours spent far from thee,
Less than the need thou hast in life of me.
                    Even less am I.

Since I, O Lord, am nothing unto thee,
See here thy Sword, I make it keen and bright,
Love's last reward, Death, comes to me to-night,
                    Farewell, Zahir-u-din.
                    Laurence Hope

NORAH

I KNEW his house by the poplar trees —
Green and silvery in the breeze;

"A heaven-high hedge," were the words he said,
"And holly-hocks — pink and white and red. ..."

It seemed so far from McChesney's Hall
Where first he told me about it all. . . .

A long path runs inside from the gate,
He still can take it early or late;

But where in the world is a path for me —
Except the river that runs to the sea!

Zoë Akins

THE MAN

The flame is spent, I can no more
Hold the tall candle by your door;
Too often have I watched to see
Your lagging steps come home to me.

The Tyrian traders taught me this:
They came perfumed with ambergris,
With amethystine robes, and hair
Curled by the kisses of salt air.

They mocked me for my weary hands
Holding your light as love demands;
They sang the lure of poppied sleep,
Their lips were warm, their eyes were deep.

The flame is spent — your pale, weak face
Must seek another resting place;
Win me and hold me now who can —
The Tyrian trader was a man.

Helen Hay Whitney

121

"UNDER DUSKY LAUREL LEAF"

UNDER dusky laurel leaf,
  Scarlet leaf of rose,
I lie prone, who have known
  All a woman knows —

Love and grief and motherhood,
  Fame and mirth and scorn;
These are all shall befall
  Any woman born.

Jewel-laden are my hands,
  Tall my stone above;
Do not weep that I sleep
  Who was wise in love;

Where I walk a shadow gray
  Through gray asphodel,
I am glad, who have had
  All that Life could tell.

Margaret Widdemer

THE LAND O' THE LEAL

I 'M wearin' awa', John,
Like snaw-wreaths in thaw, John,
I 'm wearin' awa'
    To the land o' the leal.
There 's nae sorrow there, John,
There 's neither cauld nor care, John,
The day is aye fair
    In the land o' the leal.

Our bonnie bairn 's there, John,
She was baith gude and fair, John;
And O! we grudged her sair
    To the land o' the leal.
But sorrow's sel' wears past, John,
And joy 's a-coming fast, John,
The joy that 's aye to last
    In the land o' the leal.

Sae dear 's the joy was bought, John,
Sae free the battle fought, John,
That sinfu' man e'er brought
    To the land o' the leal.

THE ANSWERING VOICE

O, dry your glistening e'e, John!
My saul langs to be free, John,
And angels beckon me
  To the land o' the leal.

O, haud ye leal and true, John!
Your day it's wearin' through, John,
And I'll welcome you
  To the land o' the leal.
Now fare-ye-weel, my ain John,
This warld's cares are vain, John,
We'll meet, and we'll be fain,
  In the land o' the leal.

Carolina, Lady Nairne

REMEMBRANCE

Cold in the earth — and the deep snow piled
    above thee,
  Far, far removed, cold in the dreary grave!
Have I forgot, my only Love, to love thee,
  Sever'd at last by Time's all-severing wave?

Now, when alone, do my thoughts no longer
    hover
  Over the mountains, on that northern shore,
Resting their wings where heath and fern-leaves
    cover
  Thy noble heart for ever, ever more?

Cold in the earth — and fifteen wild Decembers
  From those brown hills have melted into
    spring:
Faithful, indeed, is the spirit that remembers
  After such years of change and suffering!

Sweet Love of youth, forgive, if I forget thee,
  While the world's tide is bearing me along;
Other desires and other hopes beset me,
  Hopes which obscure, but cannot do thee
    wrong!

The Answering Voice

No later light has lighten'd up my heaven,
  No second morn has ever shone for me;
All my life's bliss from thy dear life was given,
  All my life's bliss is in the grave with thee.

But when the days of the golden dreams had
        perish'd,
  And even Despair was powerless to destroy;
Then did I learn how existence could be
        cherish'd,
  Strengthen'd and fed without the aid of joy.

Then did I check the tears of useless passion —
  Wean'd my young soul from yearning after
        thine;
Sternly denied its burning wish to hasten
  Down to that tomb already more than mine.

And, even yet, I dare not let it languish,
  Dare not indulge in memory's rapturous pain;
Once drinking deep of that divinest anguish,
  How could I seek the empty world again?

                                    Emily Brontë

PART TWO

LIKE A CLOUD, LIKE A MIST

COME to me out of the dark,
Like a cloud, like a mist;
Come to me out of the dark,
Silent, unseen and unknown;
Out of the darkness come
And into the darkness vanish,
Like a cloud, like a mist.

Darkness shall cover our thoughts
And cover our eyes with content,
And the sight that is of day,
And the knowledge that is of day,
Shall not have power to trouble
The delight of the lips.
Come to me out of the dark.

Come to me out of the dark
Like a cloud, like a mist;
And yet be man too, and flesh,
With arms strong to take me,
With fingers trembling to touch me,
Hands trembling at my breast.

THE ANSWERING VOICE

Have me with awe and grace
And mystery of the dark,
Unseen and unknown,
Have me with awe and grace
And freedom of the dark . . .
With dim exquisite touch . . .

Come to me out of the dark,
O love unseen and unknown,
O burdenless and unrequiring . . .
Out of the darkness come —

And into the darkness vanish —
Like a cloud, like a mist.

Helen Hoyt

SEQUENCE

ONE of these men will find my skeleton;
To one it will be delicate and slim,
With stars for eyes, and portent of a sun
Rising between the ribs to frighten him;
Yet, being bold, he might embrace it soon
With quick insensate passion in the night,
And by the holy taper of the moon
Encouraged, and because its bones were light
As filagree of pearl, he might depart
Bearing my jangled heart-strings on his heart.

And he might bury it in sand or sod,
Stamping it down to circumvent the wolf,
And, being kind, commend it to his God,
Whose Mind was swimming somewhere in the
   gulf
Above his head; but if that other found
The rotten framework of his servitor,
He'd leave it lying on the cluttered ground
Between a bottle and an apple-core,
And go his way, in agony and sweat,
Because he could not pity nor forget.

131

THE ANSWERING VOICE

II

For various questions which I shall not ask,
And various answers which I cannot hear,
I have contrived a substituted task
To prove my body is devoid of fear;
To prove my spirit's elemental blood
Is pure, courageous, and uniform,
I shall submerge my body in the mud,
I shall submit my spirit to the storm;
I shall bend down my bosom to the snake,
As to an infant for its father's sake.

I shall persist, I shall pursue my way
Believing that his cruelty was fine
As tempered steel for chastening of clay,
Impatient of corrosions that were mine;
He that despised me shall not be forgot;
He that disparaged me shall be my lord;
That was a flambeau, half-consumed and hot,
This was the running light along a sword;
And though I warmed my fingers at the one,
The other is my father and my son.

Elinor Wylie

CHERISH YOU THEN THE HOPE I SHALL FORGET

CHERISH you then the hope I shall forget
At length, my lord, Pieria? — put away
For your so passing sake, this mouth of clay,
These mortal bones against my body set,
For all the puny fever and frail sweat
Of human love, — renounce for these, I say,
The Singing Mountain's memory, and betray
The silent lyre that hangs upon me yet?
Ah, but indeed, some day shall you awake,
Rather, from dreams of me, that at your side
So many nights, a lover and a bride,
But stern in my soul's chastity, have lain,
To walk the world forever for my sake,
And in each chamber find me gone again!

Edna St. Vincent Millay

SEA LOVE

TIDE be runnin' the great world over:
   'Twas only last June month I mind that we
Was thinkin' the toss and the call in the breast
      of the lover
   So everlastin' as the sea.

Heer's the same little fishes that sputter and
      swim,
   Wi' the moon's old glim on the grey, wet sand;
An' him no more to me nor me to him
   Than the wind goin' over my hand.

Charlotte Mew

THE DROWNÈD LOVER

As I was a-walking upon my wedding-day
I met my drownèd lover who stood and barred
      my way —
"Oh! wherefore are you standing all dripping on
      the quay,
I thought you soundly sleeping ten fathoms
      deep at sea!"

I saw my drownèd lover, quite close I saw him
      stand,
His hands and face and hair and coat all black
      and caked with sand,
All dripping, rough and weedy — but not a word
      he said,
Just stood and stared with blinded eyes a-start-
      ing from his head.

"Oh! Tom! I loved you dearly, I could not
      love you more,
But there's no sense in drownèd men come float-
      ing to the shore;

The Answering Voice

And must a maid go creeping through all her
    days alone,
Whilst fathoms deep her lover lies cold as any
    stone?"

Now, is it not a hard thing the day I am to wed,
To have my drownèd lover come walking from
    the dead,
All rough and black and weedy, with tangles in
    his hair,
And not a word to wish me luck, but eyes that
    stare and stare?

"Oh! lover, drownèd lover, I loved you very
    well,
But all drowned lovers in the world can't drown
    the wedding-bell!
I'm not yet two-and-twenty, a maid can't always
    weep,
Go sleep in those deep waters as drownèd men
    should sleep!"

Lady Margaret Sackville

TWO LOVERS

MIRANDA'S lover sees himself
    A shield about her tender form;
He sees Miranda as a thing
    Too frail to brave a storm.
Miranda sees herself the stone
    Securely settled at his heart:
Were not his fibres woven there
    His body and soul would fly apart.

I see them both as gentle wraiths
    Blown by the wind, so dry, so light;
Their souls like fireflies in the dark
    Are piteously small and bright.
They are the victims of the world;
    They show no terror, no surprise:
But anyone who runs may read
    Disaster in their eyes.

Aline Kilmer

TWILIT REVELATION

This hour was set the time for heaven's descent
Come drooping toward us on the heavy air,
The sky, that's heaven's seat above us bent,
Blue faint as violet-ash, you near me there
In nether space so drenched in goblin blue,
I could touch Hesperus as soon as you.

Now I perceive you lapt in singling light,
Washed by that blue which sucks whole planets
      in,
And hung like those top jewels of the night,
A mournful gold too high for love to win.
And you, poor brief, poor melting star, you seem
Half sunk, and half to brighten in that stream.

And these rich-bodied hours of our delight
Show like a moth-wing's substance when the fall
Of confine-loosing, blue unending night
Extracts the spirit of this temporal.
So space can pierce the crevice wide between
Fast hearts, skies deep-descended intervene.

Léonie Adams

VELVET SHOES

Let us walk in the white snow
  In a soundless space;
With footsteps quiet and slow,
  At a tranquil pace,
  Under veils of white lace.

I shall go shod in silk,
  And you in wool,
White as a white cow's milk,
  More beautiful
  Than the breast of a gull.

We shall walk through the still town
  In a windless peace;
We shall step upon white down,
  Upon silver fleece,
  Upon softer than these.

We shall walk in velvet shoes:
  Wherever we go
Silence will fall like dews
  On white silence below.
  We shall walk in the snow.

Elinor Wylie

THE SNOW-GARDENS

LIKE an empty stage
The gardens are empty and cold;
The marble terraces rise
Like vases that hold no flowers;
The lake is frozen, the fountain still;
The marble walls and the seats
Are useless and beautiful.
Ah here
Where the wind and the dusk and the snow are
All is silent and white and sad.
Why do I think of you?
Why does your name remorselessly
Strike through my heart?
Why do I seem to hear
Cries as lovely as music?
Surely you never came
Into these pale snow-gardens;
Surely you never stood
Here in the twilight with me;
Yet here have I lingered and dreamed

The Snow-Gardens

Of a face as subtle as music,
Of lips that smile oddly, and eyes
Like a child's.
I have felt on my brow
Your finger-tips plaintive as music . . .
Oh, wonder of all wonders!   Oh, love —
Wrought of sweet sounds and of dreaming,
Why do you not emerge
From the lilac-pale petals of dusk
And come to me here in the gardens
Where the wind and the snow are?
Beauty and peace are here
And unceasing music,
And a loneliness chill and wistful
With the feeling of death . . .

Like a crystal lily, a star
Leans from its leaves of silver
And gleams in the sky,
And golden and faint in the shadows
You wait indistinctly,
Like a phantom lamp that appears
In the mirror of distance that hovers
By the window at twilight.

THE ANSWERING VOICE

You have come, and we stand together
With questioning eyes,
Dreaming and cold and ghostly,
In an empty garden —
Like an empty stage . . .

Zoë Akins

BY THE LAKE

Across the thick and the pastel snow
Two people go. . . . "And do you remember
When last we wandered this shore?" . . . "Ah
    no!
For it is cold-hearted December."

"Dead, the leaves that like asses' ears hung on
    the trees;
When last we wandered and squandered joy here;
Now Midas your husband will listen for these
Whispers — these tears for joy's bier."

And as they walk, they seem tall pagodas;
And all the ropes let down from the cloud
Ring the hard cold bell-buds upon the trees —
    codas
Of overtones, ecstasies, grown for love's shroud.
Edith Sitwell

HIS FIRST LOVE

CAN you forego me?   Treat me like a thing
More trivial than a flower, and less dear?
Think for a while.   Can you forego the spring,
Forfeit the one mad weather of the year?
I press between you and each yesterday;
Smelling of wind, of white brier in the dew,
From the grave's edge, and from the shrill, trod-
      den way,
I that am ghost, reach to the ghost in you.
Foregoing spring, you thus can forego me,
And bare of me, of spring you shall go bare.
Leave me or choose me.   Yet it matters not.
I shall possess you as the root the tree;
Take of your candlelight and loaf my share;
Read in your books, dig in your garden plot.

Lizette Woodworth Reese

RELEASE

I WILL not sob myself to sleep, nor waken
With tears upon my lashes; night will shelter
No wild abandonment of grief; my weeping
Shall not disturb you.

Against my burning eyelids I will fasten
The lovely image of your youthful mistress
Until at daybreak, having passed Golgotha
I shall release you.

Margaret Tod Ritter

PARTING AFTER A QUARREL

You looked at me with eyes grown bright with
      pain
Like some trapped thing's. And then you
      moved your head
Slowly from side to side, as though the strain
Ached in your throat with anger and with dread.

And then you turned and left me, and I stood
With a queer sense of deadness over me,
And only wondered dully that you could
Fasten your trench-coat up so carefully

Till you were gone. Then all the air was thick
With my last words that seemed to leap and
      quiver.
And in my heart I heard the little click
Of a door that closes — quietly, forever.

Eunice Tietjens

THE HAUNTED HEART

I AM not wholly yours, for I can face
    A world without you in the years to be,
    And think of love that has been given me
By other men, and wear it as a grace;
Yes, even in your arms there is a space
    That yet might widen to infinity,
    And deep within your eyes I still can see
Old memories that I cannot erase.

But let these ghostly tenants of the heart
    Stay on unchallenged through the changing
        days
    And keep their shadowy leaseholds without
        fear,
Then if the hour should come when we must
        part,
    We know that we shall go on haunted ways,
    Each to the end inalienably dear.

Jessie B. Rittenhouse

BEFORE YOU CAME

BEFORE you came
A word you said
Ran through my days
Like living flame.

It was not you —
It was a name
For loveliness . . .
And yet it drew

Your Self for me
So that I knew
Your mood, your smile,
All you must be.

Oh, long ago
I dreamed you so —
Subtle as flame,

And cold as frost,
And mine, and lost
Before you came.

Marjorie Meeker

ST. CLARE HEARS ST. FRANCIS

FRANCIS was preaching in the lazarhouse court-
      yard
  On lifting the Host.
I thought he looked exceeding like the Saviour
  Or the Holy Ghost.

He said the sacred Host was sunk and neglected
  Wherever man's heart was bowed.
"Let us lift the heart of man, and the Host will
      be lifted!"
  Francis cried aloud.

I stood there drinking up cupfulls of his greatness
  And of his joy.
I remembered him dancing all along the Piazza
  When he was a boy.

I was loving his hands, and his bare feet, and his
      shadow,
  And the leper on whom it fell.
I was wishing for some rough work to do for the
      lepers,
  To serve them well.

THE ANSWERING VOICE

I did not hope that he knew I was standing near
      him,
  Nor wonder if by long prayer
I could make my love creep into his great horizon
  Like a current of air.

Back over me came flooding my love for Francis,
  Which, when I pray,
By an act of love for all poor desolate people,
  I fling and scatter away.

I disappeared from my thoughts, from my own
      sensation;
  Nothing was there
But a fire of sweetness following after Francis,
  From the ashes of Clare.

Sarah N. Cleghorn

THE MAID'S TRAGEDY

I KEPT two singing birds
In a cage of bone —
Hatched-out on the same day;
But since one flew away,
T'other's alone.

I spoke him gentle words
And bade him sing.
But he hung down his head
As if discomforted,
And drooped his wing.

My mood was turned to rage;
I stinted his seed,
Opened the cage-door wide —
Starve, or begone! I cried.
He did not heed.

Silent within his cage
I see him mope
Like any turtle-dove.
The dumb bird I called Love,
The flown bird, Hope.

Sylvia Townsend Warner

ELAINE

OH, come again to Astolat!
  I will not ask you to be kind.
And you may go when you will go,
  And I will stay behind.

I will not say how dear you are,
  Or ask you if you hold me dear,
Or trouble you with things for you
  The way I did last year.

So still the orchard, Lancelot,
  So very still the lake shall be,
You could not guess — though you should
    guess —
  What is become of me.

So wide shall be the garden-walk,
  The garden-seat so very wide,
You needs must think — if you should think —
  The lily maid had died.

152

Elaine

Save that, a little way away,
   I 'd watch you for a little while,
To see you speak, the way you speak,
   And smile, — if you should smile.

Edna St. Vincent Millay

MEN LOVED WHOLLY BEYOND WISDOM

MEN loved wholly beyond wisdom
Have the staff without the banner.
Like a fire in a dry thicket
Rising within women's eyes
Is the love men must return.
Heart, so subtle now, and trembling,
What a marvel to be wise,
To love never in this manner!
To be quiet in the fern
Like a thing gone dead and still,
Listening to the prisoned cricket
Shake its terrible, dissembling
Music in the granite hill.

Louise Bogan

IN THE ORCHARD

"I thought you loved me." "No, it was only
    fun."
"When we stood there closer 'n all? . . ."
    "Well, the harvest moon
Was shining and queer in your hair, and it
    turned my head."
"That made you?" "Yes." "Just the moon
    and the light it made
Under the tree?" "Well, your mouth too . . ."
    "Yes, my mouth?"
"And the quiet there that sang like the drum in
    the booth . . .
You shouldn't have danced like that!" "Like
    what?" "So close,
With your head turned up, and the flower in
    your hair — a rose
That smelt all warm." "I loved you. I
    thought you knew
155

I would n't have danced like that with any but
    you."

"I did n't know. I thought you knew it was fun."

"I thought it was love you meant." "Well, it's
    done."

        "Yes, it 's done.

I 've seen boys stone a blackbird, and watched
    them drown

A kitten . . . it clawed at the reeds and they
    pushed it down

Into the pool while it screamed. Is that fun
    too ?"

"Well . . . boys are like that . . . your broth-
    ers . . ." "Yes, I know,

But you, so lovely and strong! Not you! Not
    you !"

"They don't understand it 's cruel. It 's only
    a game."

"And are girls fun too ?" "No, still, in a way
    it 's the same.

It 's queer and lovely to have a girl . . ." "Go
    on . . ."

"It makes you mad for a bit to feel she 's your
    own,

In the Orchard

And you laugh and kiss her, and maybe you give
  her a ring,
But it's only in fun." "But I gave you every-
  thing."
"Well, you shouldn't have done it. You know
  what a fellow thinks
When a girl does that." "Yes, he talks of her
  over his drinks
And calls her a — " "Stop that now. I
  thought you knew."
"But it wasn't with anyone else, it was only
  you."
"How did I know? I thought you wanted it
  too.
I thought you were like the rest . . . Well,
  what's to be done?"
"To be done?" "Is it all right?" "Yes."
  "Sure?" "Yes, but why?"
"I don't know. I thought you were going to
  cry.
You said you had something to tell me." "Yes,
  I know,
It wasn't anything really . . . I think I'll
  go."

The Answering Voice

"Yes, it's late.   There's thunder about, a drop
   of rain
Fell on my hand in the dark.   I'll see you again
At the dance next week . . . You're sure that
   everything's right?"
"Yes."   "Well, I'll be going."   "Kiss me . . ."
   "Goodnight" . . . "Goodnight."

Muriel Stuart

PAGEANT

THOUGH I go by with banners,
  Oh, never envy me
These flags of scarlet flying,
  This purple that you see. . . .

This air of marching triumph
  Was all that I could save
Of loves that had an ending
  And hopes that had a grave.
                    Margaret Widdemer

ESTABLISHED

I MADE a house of houselessness,
    A garden of your going:
And seven trees of seven wounds
    You gave me, all unknowing:
I made a feast of golden grief
    That you so lordly left me,
I made a bed of all the smiles
    Whereof your lips bereft me:
I made a sun of your delay,
    Your daily loss, his setting:
I made a wall of all your words
    And a lock of your forgetting.

Rose O'Neill

THE LETTER

LITTLE cramped words scrawling all over the
    paper
Like draggled fly's legs,
What can you tell of the flaring moon
Through the oak leaves?
Or of my uncurtained window and the bare floor
Spattered with moonlight?
Your silly quirks and twists have nothing in
    them
Of blossoming hawthorns,
And this paper is dull, crisp, smooth, virgin of
    loveliness
Beneath my hand.

I am tired, Beloved, of chafing my heart against
The want of you;
Of squeezing it into little inkdrops,
And posting it.
And I scald alone, here, under the fire
Of the great moon.

Amy Lowell

SONG

LOVE me because I am lost;
Love me that I am undone.
That is brave, — no man has wished **it,**
Not one.

Be strong, to look on my heart
As others look on my face.
Love me, — I tell you that it is a ravaged
Terrible place.

Louise Bogan

A MEMORY

I REMEMBER
The crackle of the palm trees
Over the mooned white roofs of the town . . .
The shining town . . .
And the tender fumbling of the surf
On the sulphur-yellow beaches
As we sat . . . a little apart . . . in the close-
pressing night.

The moon hung above us like a golden mango,
And the moist air clung to our faces,
Warm and fragrant as the open mouth of a child
And we watched the out-flung sea
Rolling to the purple edge of the world,
Yet ever back upon itself . . .
As we . . .

Inadequate night . . .
And mooned white memory
Of a tropic sea . . .
How softly it comes up
Like an ungathered lily.

Lola Ridge

I DO REMEMBER YOU

I DO remember you as music toned —
The lowest notes upon the deepest string —
And a great strength along them, like a vow.

I do remember you as light that floods
Through dust-beams, mellow to the empty
      aisles —
Shaft from some high, some confident window
      place,
Where all the rest have darkened, one by one.

Roberta Teale Swartz

TO ———

WHEN I grow old and my quick blood is chilled,
And all my thoughts are grey as my grey hair,
When I am slow and dull, and do not care,
And all the strife and storm of Life are stilled;
Then if one carelessly should speak your name
It will go through my body like swift spears
To set my fireless bosom in a flame,
My faded eyelids will be bright with tears;
And I shall find how far my heart has gone
From wanting you, — how lost and long ago
That love of ours was: I shall suddenly know
How old and grey I am . . . and how alone.

                                    Muriel Stuart

I HAVE BEEN THROUGH THE GATES

His heart, to me, was a place of palaces and
    pinnacles and shining towers;
I saw it then as we see things in dreams, — I do
    not remember how long I slept;
I remember the trees, and the high, white walls,
    and how the sun was always on the
    towers;
The walls are standing to-day, and the gates: I
    have been through the gates, I have
    groped, I have crept
Back, back. There is dust in the streets, and
    blood; they are empty; darkness is over
    them;
His heart is a place with the lights gone out, for-
    saken by great winds and the heavenly
    rain, unclean and unswept,
Like the heart of the holy city, old, blind, beauti-
    ful Jerusalem,
        Over which Christ wept.

Charlotte Mew

THE UNFAITHFUL

Break me a bread not made with hands,
And I will eat and never more
Go wandering forth in foreign lands
Looking — what am I looking for?

Or teach me how to brew my own
Drink, and how to make such bread;
Others, asked, have offered a stone —
You must give me myself, instead.

And I will thus reward your love:
Never to eat of you again,
And stand alone, and never move,
And look like rock — to other men.

(Too hollow for you to ask much of,
But a rock to anchor other men.)

Genevieve Taggard

167

BALLAD OF THE RAG–BAG HEART

I WISH my heart
    Were a golden cup
So love might come
    And fill it up,

Or like a sieve
    Of shiny tin,
That not a drop
    Could linger in!

From what I know
    My heart, perhaps,
Is a patch-work rag-bag
    Filled with scraps,

So tightly crammed,
    So rudely tossed,
So carelessly rummaged
    That much is lost.

With sample and snippet,
    With piece and part,
Fie on the woman
    With such a heart!

Ballad of the Rag-Bag Heart

How simple, how noble
It were to live
With a heart like a cup
Or a bright tin sieve!

Marjorie Allen Seiffert

DIAGONALS

Now this is the strangest thing since the world
        began :
You tell me that you are a bad and a violent
        man ;
  But I see only
  A child, little and lonely,
Crying with fright in a desolate place apart.

While I am known as chaste and reasonably
        good :
But you are blind to my virtuous womanhood ;
  Somehow you see,
  Dragged out of the depths of me,
The wanton that every woman hides in her
        heart.

Aline Kilmer

YOU MAKE ME THINK OF LOOPS OF
WATER LYING

You make me think of loops of water lying:
Of the blue heron dusk among the reeds:
Of mornings when the windy clouds are flying
And love is the last thing your spirit needs:
Of bitterness that you are still denying:
Of the pomegranate's sharp cornelian seeds:
And of those porcelain-hollow tinkling creeds
That torture you till there is no replying.
You are not of those who wonder or care to ask
More of a woman than the moment's grace.
What she may know of love concerns you little.
Let her adjust the bright deliberate mask
And do her thinking in some lonely place
Meant to convince her heart that love is brittle.

Grace Hazard Conkling

LOVE SONG FROM NEW ENGLAND

In every solemn tree the wind
   Has rung a little lonesome bell,
As sweet and clear, as cool and kind
   As my voice bidding you farewell.

This is an hour that gods have loved
   To snatch with bare, bright hands and hold.
Mine, with a gesture, grey and gloved,
   Dismiss it from me in the cold.

Closely as some dark-shuttered house
   I keep my light.   How should you know,
That as you turn beneath brown boughs,
   My heart is breaking in the snow?

Winifred Welles

SONG FOR UNBOUND HAIR

Oh, never marry Ishmael.
Marry another and prosper well;
But not, but never Ishmael . . .

What has he ever to buy or sell?
He only owns what his strength can keep,
Only a vanishing knot of sheep,
A goat or two.   Does he sow or reap?
In the hanging rocks rings his old ram's bell —
Who would marry Ishmael!

What has he to give to a bride?
Only trouble, little beside,
Only his arm like a little cave
To cover a woman and keep her safe;
A rough fierce kiss, and the wind and the rain,
A child, perhaps, and another again —
Who would marry Ishmael?

The Answering Voice

The arrogant Lucifer when he fell
Bequeathed his wrath to Ishmael;
The hand of every man is set
Against this lad, and this lad's hand
Is cruel and quick, — forget, forget
The nomad boy on his leagues of sand. . . .

Marry another and prosper well,
But not, but never Ishmael.

Genevieve Taggard

THE FARMER'S WIFE

He will not hear the cuckoo call,
The last faint snow will seal his eyes.
I shall see a lone star fall
Above the bare pine ere he dies.

My own heart and the clock will soon
Alone keep all the silence here —
Unless the foolish, crying loon
Or the chanting wind come near.

He will not hold the soil again
In his two hands, nor will his face
Lift to the power of the rain
That early April brings this place.

To the south his orchard lies,
His naked wheat-field to the west,
And well will *they* know when he dies
He loved me only second best.

Martha Ostenso

THE ISLANDS

I

WHAT are the islands to me,
what is Greece,
what is Rhodes, Samos, Chios,
what is Paros facing west,
what is Crete?

What is Samothrace,
rising like a ship,
what is Imbros rending the storm-waves
with its breast?

What is Naxos, Paros, Milos,
what the circle about Lycia,
what, the Cyclades'
white necklace?

What is Greece —
Sparta, rising like a rock,
Thebes, Athens,
what is Corinth?

THE ISLANDS

What is Euboia
with its island violets,
what is Euboia, spread with grass,
set with swift shoals,
what is Crete?

What are the islands to me,
what is Greece?

II

What can love of land give to me
that you have not —
what do the tall Spartans know,
and gentler Attic folk?

What has Sparta and her women
more than this?

What are the islands to me
if you are lost —
what is Naxos, Tinos, Andros,
and Delos, the clasp
of the white necklace?

The Answering Voice

III

What can love of land give to me
that you have not,
what can love of strife break in me
that you have not?

Though Sparta enter Athens,
Thebes wrack Sparta,
each changes as water,
salt, rising to wreak terror
and fall back.

IV

"What has love of land given to you
that I have not?"

I have questioned Tyrians
where they sat
on the black ships,
weighted with rich stuffs,
I have asked the Greeks
from the white ships,
and Greeks from ships whose hulks
lay on the wet sand, scarlet

THE ISLANDS

with great beaks.
I have asked bright Tyrians
and tall Greeks —
"what has love of land given you ?"
And they answered — "peace."

v

But Beauty is set apart,
beauty is cast by the sea,
a barren rock,
beauty is set about
with wrecks of ships,
upon our coast, death keeps
the shallows — death waits
clutching toward us
from the deeps.

Beauty is set apart;
the winds that slash its beach,
swirl the coarse sand
upward toward the rocks.
Beauty is set apart
from the islands
and from Greece.

The Answering Voice

VI

In my garden
the winds have beaten
the ripe lilies;
in my garden, the salt
has wilted the first flakes
of young narcissus,
and the lesser hyacinth,
and the salt has crept
under the leaves of the white hyacinth.
In my garden
even the wind-flowers lie flat,
broken by the wind at last.

VII

What are the islands to me
if you are lost,
what is Paros to me
if your eyes draw back,
what is Milos
if you take fright of beauty,
terrible, torturous, isolated,
a barren rock?

The Islands

What is Rhodes, Crete,
what is Paros facing west,
what, white Imbros?

What are the islands to me
if you hesitate,
what is Greece if you draw back
from the terror
and cold splendour of song
and its bleak sacrifice?

H. D.

SHE SAYS, BEING FORBIDDEN:

AND was there not a king somewhere who said:
"Back, waves! I do command you!" I forget
His name, beloved, or his race, and yet
I know the story and am comforted.
The tides will rise, are rising — see, they spread
About your robes, your ermine will be wet,
Your velvet shoes, your dear dear feet! Ah let
Me warn you, sir, the waves will reach your
      head!

My king, my kingly love, how shall we stay
The bold broad lifting of this lovely sea?
What is the master word that we must say
To bring these roaring waters to the knee?
The other king went scampering away!
Will you so do? Or will you drown with me?
                  Leonora Speyer

THE LOVE–SONG

I AM more tall today than ever before;
So great is my pride, as I sing aloud your song,
That the city street seems like the deck of a ship
Breasting far waves of cloud.   The world moves
       thus
Out on its seas of air to the tune of your song,
Rising and falling under the straight noon sun.

You would never know your song, I am shouting
       it so,
But shouting is fine, when the waves of the sea
       run high!
Loud notes flung to the wind and carried away
Down through the shining water and shining air!
Shouting is fine, when a ship moves under your
       feet,
And all of your being is full of remembered song!

I am so tall today!   I can almost forget
Your notes were made for another, and not for me;
And sung in the quiet dark with a voice that
       trembled . . .

The Answering Voice

Now from afar, and under the deep noon sky,
I do not care to know if she understood. . .
Let there be shouting — shouting into the sun !

For to all the world the street is only the street
Where one may pass who sings that her heart is
    full ;
And none must know that the street is plunging
    before me,
Downward and down to the constant rhythm of
    singing, —
Sucked to the whirlpool dark in the surging of
    music, —
Rudderless, — lost, — in the song that is not
    forgotten.

Bernice Lesbia Kenyon

DAWN

So begins the day,
Solid, chill, and gray,
But my heart will wake
Happy for your sake;
No more tossed and wild,
Singing like a child,
Quiet as a flower
In this first gray hour.

So my heart will wake
Happy, for your sake.

Frances Cornford

THANKS TO MY WORLD FOR THE LOAN OF A FAIR DAY

That day you wrought for me
Shone, and was ended.
Perfect your thought for me,
Whom you befriended.
Such joy was new to me —
New, and most splendid,
More than was due to me.
More than was due to me.

Though I do wrong to you
Having no power,
Singing no song to you,
Bringing no flower,
Yet does my youth again
Thrill, for the hour
Cometh in truth again.
Cometh in truth again.

THANKS TO MY WORLD

I shall possess to-day
All I have wanted,
All I lacked yesterday
Now shall be granted.
No longer dumb to you,
Changed and enchanted,
Singing I'll come to you.
Singing I'll come to you.

I will amass for you
Very great treasure.
Swift years shall pass for you
Dancing for pleasure.
Time shall be slave to me,
Giving — full measure —
All that you gave to me.
All that you gave to me.

Stella Benson

A SONG FOR MY MATE

HIGHER than the slim eucalyptus,
Higher than the dim, purple mountains,
Higher than the stern flight of eagles,
    Rose our young hopes, long, long ago.

Sweeter than wild, sweet berries,
Sweeter than a chill spring's bounty,
Sweeter than a meadowlark's carol,
    Were the young, sweet joys that we shared.

More bitter than a swelling olive,
More bitter than a brackish river,
More bitter than a crow's hard laughter,
    Were the sorrows we have known, my dear.

But nearer than the light is to the day,
And nearer than the night is to darkness,
And nearer than the winds to their crooning,
    I am drawn, I am held to your heart.

                              Marguerite Wilkinson

HOMAGE

Before me you bowed as before an altar,
And I reached down and drew you to my bosom;
Proud of your reverence, and reverence return-
ing,
But craving most your love and not your awe.

My hands about your head curved themselves
as holding
A treasure, fragile and of glad possession;
Dear were the bones of your skull beneath my
fingers,
And I grew brave at thought of your defense.

Not as a man I felt you in my brooding,
But as a babe, a babe of my own body;
Precious your worth, but dearer your depend-
ence;
Almost I wished to feed you at my breast.

The Answering Voice

And not to me, I knew, belonged your homage:
I but the vessel of your holy drinking;
The channel to you of that ancient wonder
Of love and womanhood, I but a woman.

Then never need your memory be shamefaced
That I have seen your flesh and soul at worship;
Do you think I did not kneel when you were
    kneeling?
Even lowlier bowed my head, and bowed my
    heart.

Helen Hoyt

THE ANCIENT BEAUTIFUL THINGS

I AM all alone in the room.
The evening stretches before me
Like a road all delicate gloom
Till it reaches the midnight's gate.
And I hear his step on the path,
And his questioning whistle, low
At the door as I hurry to meet him.

He will ask, 'Are the doors all locked?
Is the fire made safe on the hearth?
And she — is she sound asleep?'

I shall say, 'Yes, the doors are locked,
And the ashes are white as the frost:
Only a few red eyes
To stare at the empty room.
And she is all sound asleep,
Up there where the silence sings,
And the curtains stir in the cold.'

THE ANSWERING VOICE

He will ask, 'And what did you do
While I have been gone so long?
So long! Four hours or five!'
I shall say, 'There was nothing I did. —

I mended that sleeve of your coat.
And I made her a little white hood
Of the furry pieces I found
Up in the garret to-day.
She shall wear it to play in the snow,
Like a little white bear — and shall laugh,
And tumble, and crystals of stars
Shall shine on her cheeks and hair. —
It was nothing I did. — I thought
You would never come home again!'

Then he will laugh out, low,
Being fond of my folly, perhaps;
And softly and hand in hand
We shall creep upstairs in the dusk,
To look at her, lying asleep:
Our little gold bird in her nest;
The wonderful bird who flew in
At the window our life flung wide.

THE ANCIENT BEAUTIFUL THINGS

(How should we have chosen her,
Had we seen them all in a row,
The unborn vague little souls,
All wings and tremulous hands?
How should we have chosen her,
Made like a star to shine,
Made like a bird to fly,
Out of a drop of our blood,
And earth, and fire, and God?)

Then we shall go to sleep,
Glad. —
        O God, did you know
When you moulded men out of clay,
Urging them up and up
  Through the endless circles of change,
Travail and turmoil and death,
Many would curse you down,
Many would live all gray
With their faces flat like a mask?
But there would be some, O God,
Crying to you each night,
'I am so glad! so glad!
I am so rich and gay!
How shall I thank you, God?'

THE ANSWERING VOICE

Was that one thing you knew
When you smiled and found it was good:
The curious teeming earth
That grew like a child at your hand?
Ah, you might smile, for that! —

I am all alone in the room.
The books and the pictures peer,
Dumb old friends, from the dark.
The wind goes high on the hills,
And my fire leaps out, being proud.
The terrier, down on the hearth,
Twitches and barks in his sleep,
Soft little foolish barks,
More like a dream than a dog. —

I will mend the sleeve of that coat,
All ragged — and make her the hood,
Furry, and white, for the snow.
She shall tumble and laugh. —
                                    Oh, I think,
Though a thousand rivers of grief
Flood over my head, — though a hill
Of horror lie on my breast, —
Something will sing, 'Be glad!

The Ancient Beautiful Things

You have had all your heart's desire:
The unknown things that you asked
When you lay awake in the nights,
Alone, and searching the dark
For the secret wonder of life.
You have had them (can you forget?),
The ancient beautiful things!' . . .

How long he is gone!   And yet
It is only an hour or two. . . .

Oh, I am so happy!   My eyes
Are troubled with tears.
                              Did you know,
Oh, God, they would be like this,
Your ancient beautiful things?
Are there more?   Are there more — out there? —
O God, are there always more?

                              Fannie Stearns Davis

195

MARRIAGE

NOT any more, not ever while I live
With you, shall I be single or be whole.
A wife is one who cannot cease to give
Flowers of her body, and graftings from her soul.

I came to bud for you like a young tree;
And though I should not give you any fruit,
Here is one orchard where your hands make free.
Something is always tugging at my root.

Though you abandon what you once found sweet,
I shall be like a birch whose bark is torn
By fingers scratching difficult, incomplete
Confessions of an outlived love and scorn.

And though I wither near you, patiently
As any bough that any wind can break,
You will go on having as much of me
As winter from a stricken limb can take.

You are my winter, as you are my spring.
However we pretend, this will be true.
You are the wind that makes the leafage sing
And strips the branches that it quivers through.

Babette Deutsch

196

BENVENUTO'S VALENTINE

Not for the child that wanders home
So wasted by barbaric kings,
So wearied by imperial Rome,
That he will clasp my apron-strings.

Not for the ghost that never is
And never will be known by me,
Whose heel is on the precipice
Before its print has left the sea.

And not for darling Harlequin
Spinning in stars of diamond shape;
Nor Hamlet exquisite and thin
As moonbeams in an inky cape.

Not for the legend latest-born
Of Chivalry and Virgin, whom
Roland has knighted with a horn,
And Richard with a sprig of broom.

The Answering Voice

Not even for the man who climbed
A thousand miles to thrust a torch
Among forgotten fagots, rimed
By winter in an iron porch.

But for the thought, that wrought and planned
Such intricate and crystal things,
My kiss is set upon your hand
As softly as a silver ring's.

Elinor Wylie

THE MEETING

WE started speaking,
Looked at each other, then turned away.
The tears kept rising to my eyes
But I could not weep.
I wanted to take your hand
But my hand trembled.
You kept counting the days
Before we should meet again.
But both of us felt in our hearts
That we parted for ever and ever.
   The ticking of the little clock filled the quiet
      room.
"Listen," I said.   "It is so loud,
Like a horse galloping on a lonely road,
As loud as that — a horse galloping past in the
      night."
   You shut me up in your arms.
But the sound of the clock stifled our hearts'
      beating.
You said, "I cannot go: all that is living of me

Is here for ever and ever."
Then you went.
    The world changed. The sound of the clock
        grew fainter,
Dwindled away, became a minute thing.
I whispered in the darkness, "If it stops, I shall
      die."

Katherine Mansfield

EVADNE

I FIRST tasted under Apollo's lips
love and love sweetness,
I Evadne;
my hair is made of crisp violets
or hyacinth which the wind combs back
across some rock shelf;
I Evadne
was mate of the god of light.

His hair was crisp to my mouth
as the flower of the crocus,
across my cheek,
cool as the silver cress
on Erotos bank;
between my chin and throat
his mouth slipped over and over.

Still between my arm and shoulder,
I feel the brush of his hair,
and my hands keep the gold they took
as they wandered over and over
that great arm-full of yellow flowers.

H. D.

SONG OF THE LONG RIVER

ALL day my songs
Sang beside the River,
Sang on my lips like my lover's kiss.
I asked no more:
   "Tell me, how long, Sky, how long is the River
That flows on and on yet stays forever,
Bearing my songs oh whither, whither?"

I said only: —
   "When the starry wampum is offered,
When the twilight smoke signals
That the woman, Swiya, camps beneath the
     willows
And her tent of willows,
Is open — is open — open. . . .
Will he come, the Man of Arrows,
Like a white hawk skimming
Down the circling path of waters,
Down the tide
Of the silver singing River,
That winds — and, winding, beckons —
Like a low-hung girdle round the hills?"

SONG OF THE LONG RIVER

I said only:
   "Come! Swift and Wounding One, to my lips.
When the two crimson wings,
The wings of my flying Song, are folded!

The flesh of my songs is sweeter, O Wounding One,
Than wild turkeys;
Softer than feathers is Swiya's breast, swelling
      with love.

Moor thy white canoe
By the running River
Till lily-picker Dawn shall pluck it
From the black-tipped clustering bulrushes of
      night.
Leave the shallower tide
Of the silver singing River, for the deeper flowing;
Leap to the still-winged silence of thy mate!"

When the starry wampum is offered,
When the twilight smoke signals
That the woman, Swiya, camps beneath the willows;
And her tent of willows,
Red spring willows,
Is open — is open — open — . . .
                    Constance Lindsay Skinner

WHAT LIPS MY LIPS HAVE KISSED

WHAT lips my lips have kissed, and where, and
    why,
I have forgotten, and what arms have lain
Under my head till morning; but the rain
Is full of ghosts to-night, that tap and sigh
Upon the glass and listen for reply,
And in my heart there stirs a quiet pain
For unremembered lads that not again
Will turn to me at midnight with a cry.
Thus in the winter stands the lonely tree,
Nor knows what birds have vanished one by one,
Yet knows its boughs more silent than before :
I cannot say what loves have come and gone,
I only know that summer sang in me
A little while, that in me sings no more.

Edna St. Vincent Millay

LAKE–SONG

THE lapping of lake water
Is like the weeping of women,
The weeping of ancient women
Who grieved without rebellion.

The lake falls over the shore
Like tears on their curven bosoms.
Here is languid, luxurious wailing,
The wailing of kings' daughters.

So do we ever cry,
A soft, unmutinous crying,
When we know ourselves each a princess
Locked fast within her tower.

The lapping of lake water
Is like the weeping of women,
The fertile tears of women
That water the dreams of men.

Jean Starr Untermeyer

INDEXES

INDEX OF FIRST LINES

PART ONE

Across the shimmering meadows 34
After the fierce midsummer all ablaze 84
Against the planks of the cabin side . . . 73
Ah, Love, I cannot die, I cannot go . . . 77
All the ghosts I ever knew 102
Along her tranquil way she went 116
And if I came not again 54
And ye sall walk in silk attire 92
As a little child I come 40
As the mother bird to the waiting nest . . . 24
At Loschwitz above the city 2

Be not angry with me that I bear 27
Before I trust my fate to thee 47
Belovèd, my belovèd, when I think . . . 26
Bury me deep when I am dead 113

Carnations and my first love ! and he was seventeen 97
Cold in the earth — and the deep snow piled above
   thee 125
Come back to me, who wait and watch for you . 69
Could ye come back to me, Douglas, Douglas . . 114
Cover mine eyes, O my Love ! 35

Dear Love, it was so hard to say 83

Even for you I shall not weep 107

INDEX OF FIRST LINES — PART ONE

Go from me. Yet I feel that I shall stand . . . 64
Good-bye! — no, do not grieve that it is over . . 66
Grandmither, think not I forget, when I come back
    to town 108

He was straight and strong, and his eyes were blue. 118
He whistled soft whistlings I knew were for me . 14
Hill people turn to their hills 23
How do I love thee? Let me count the ways . . 43

I am the Other — I who come 86
I am the wind that wavers 80
I'm wearin' awa', John 123
I came into your room and spoke 58
I cannot always feel his greatness 37
I have always hated the rain 29
I have seen the proudest stars 3
I have wandered to a spring in the forest green and
    dim 5
I knew his house by the poplar trees 120
I leaned out my window, I smelt the white clover . 31
I love my life, but not too well 59
I love thee, dear, and knowing mine own heart . 51
I must not think of thee; and, tired yet strong . 65
I must not yield . . . but if he would not sing! . 63
I read the pain and pathos of your eyes . . . 117
I sat among the green leaves, and heard the nuts
    falling 13
I say it to comfort me over and over 72
I've learned to say it carelessly 30
I went out to the farthest meadow 8
I went to dig a grave for Love 67
I will arise and go hence to the west 10
I will not give thee all my heart 56
If I could only serve him 81

210

Index of First Lines — Part One

If thou must love me, let it be for nought . . . 41
It is so long gone by, and yet 99

Less than the dust, beneath thy Chariot wheel . . 119
Let us forget we loved each other much . . . 76
Love came back at fall o' dew 90
Love has gone and left me and the days are all
alike 70
Love me at last, or if you will not 6

Many in aftertimes will say of you 78
My Dear was a mason 36
My debt to you, Belovèd 46
My heart is like a singing bird 17
My life closed twice before its close 53

Never the nightingale 100
Now evening comes. Now stirs my discontent . 68

O my Lover, blind me 42
O strong sun of heaven, harm not my love . . . 21
Of all the souls that stand create 19
Oh, have you not a message, you who come over the
sea ? 85
Oh ! I know why the alder trees 39
Oh, maybe it was yesterday, or fifty years ago ! . 94
Oh, the burden, the burden of love ungiven . . 12
Oh, when I saw your eyes 18
Out of the window the trees in the Square . . . 7

Pines, and a blur of lithe young grasses . . . 91

Rain, rain, — fall, fall 33

So beautiful you are, indeed 20
Somewhere or other there must surely be . . . 1

211

Index of First Lines — Part One

Step lightly across the floor 111
Such special sweetness was about 52

The flame is spent, I can no more 121
The hills far-off were blue, blue 15
The love of my life came not 103
There is a strong wall about me to protect me . . 22
There is no one beside thee, and no one above thee 62
There was a garden planned in Spring's young days 11
To-day I went among the mountain folk . . . 101

Under dusky laurel leaf 122

Walk into the world 60
What good is there, ah me, what good in Love? . 75
When I am dead, my dearest 112
When I go away from you 44
When on the marge of evening the last blue light is
  broken 25
When the sheep are in the fauld, when the kye's
  come hame 104
When we shall be dust in the churchyard . . . 79
Whose doorway was it, in the sordid street . . . 88
Why didst thou come into my life so late? . . . 96

Yet for one rounded moment I will be 61
You ask me what — since we must part . . . 57
You need not say one word to me, as up the hill we
  go 49
You say there is no love, my love 45

INDEX OF FIRST LINES

PART TWO

Across the thick and the pastel snow 143
All day my songs 202
And was there not a king somewhere who said . . 182
As I was a-walking upon my wedding-day . . . 135

Before me you bowed as before an altar . . . 189
Before you came 148
Break me a bread not made with hands . . . 167

Can you forego me? Treat me like a thing . . 144
Cherish you then the hope I shall forget . . . 133
Come to me out of the dark 129

Francis was preaching in the lazarhouse courtyard . 149

He will not hear the cuckoo call 175
Higher than the slim eucalyptus 188
His heart, to me, was a place of palaces and pinnacles
and shining towers 166

I am all alone in the room 191
I am more tall today than ever before 183
I am not wholly yours for I can face 147
I do remember you as music toned 164
I first tasted under Apollo's lips 201
I kept two singing birds 151
I made a house of houselessness 160
I remember 163
"I thought you loved me." "No, it was only
fun." 155

213

INDEX OF FIRST LINES — PART TWO

I will not sob myself to sleep, nor waken . . . 145
I wish my heart 168
In every solemn tree the wind 172

Let us walk in the white snow 139
Like an empty stage 140
Little cramped words scrawling all over the paper . 161
Love me because I am lost 162

Men loved wholly beyond wisdom 154
Miranda's lover sees himself 137

Not any more, not ever while I live 196
Not for the child that wanders home 197
Now this is the strangest thing since the world
    began 170

Oh, come again to Astolat! 152
Oh, never marry Ishmael 173
One of these men will find my skeleton . . . 131

So begins the day 185

That day you wrought for me 186
The lapping of lake water 205
This hour was set the time for heaven's descent . 138
Though I go by with banners 159
Tide be runnin' the great world over 134

We started speaking 199
What are the islands to me 176
What lips my lips have kissed, and where, and
    why 204
When I grow old and my quick blood is chilled . 165

You looked at me with eyes grown bright with
    pain 146
You make me think of loops of water lying . . 171

INDEX OF AUTHORS

PART ONE

Akins, Zoë 33, 80, 120
Aldrich, Anne Reeve 67

Barker, Elsa 39
Barnard, Anne 104
Blamire, Susanna 92
Branch, Anna Hempstead 81
Brontë, Emily 125
Browning, Elizabeth Barrett . 26, 41, 43, 62, 64
Burr, Amelia Josephine 51, 118

Carbery, Ethna 86
Carolina, Lady Nairne 123
Cather, Willa Sibert 34, 108
Chesson, Nora 10
Coates, Florence Earle 24
Colby, Vine 88
Conkling, Grace Hazard 56
Corbin, Alice 6
Craik, Dinah Mulock 114
Crapsey, Adelaide 100

Dargan, Olive Tilford 101
Davies, Mary Carolyn 22
Davis, Fannie Stearns 49, 54
Dickinson, Emily 19, 53

Index of Authors — Part One

Dorr, Julia C. R. 96
Dudley, Helen 3

Ewing, Juliana Horatia 57

French, Nora May 63, 68

Garrison, Theodosia 72
Guiney, Louise Imogen 25

Harding, Ruth Guthrie 91
Hope, Laurence 73, 119
Hoyt, Helen 14

Ingelow, Jean 31

Lee, Muna 79
Levy, Amy 2, 99
Lowell, Amy 27, 44

McCourt, Edna Wahlert 5
McLeod, Irene Rutherford 20, 40
Meynell, Alice 65
Millay, Edna St. Vincent 70
Monroe, Harriet 59, 66
Murray, Ada Foster 116

Naidu, Sarojini 35
Norton, Grace Fallow 8, 12, 45

O'Neill, Moira 94

Palmer, Alice Freeman 83
Parrish, Williamina 30
Peabody, Josephine Preston 15, 18
Pickthall, Marjorie L. C. 13
Procter, Adelaide Anne 47

Index of Authors — Part One

Reese, Lizette Woodworth 52, 90, 102
Rittenhouse, Jessie B. 46
Robinson, A. Mary F. 7, 75, 76, 77
Robinson, Corinne Roosevelt 117
Rossetti, Christina 1, 17, 69, 78, 112

Sackville, Margaret 85

Thomas, Edith M. 11, 103, 111
Tietjens, Eunice 37
Tynan, Katharine 58

Untermeyer, Jean Starr 29, 60

Watson, Rosamund Marriott . . . 107, 113
Wharton, Edith 61
Whitney, Helen Hay 121
Wickham, Anna 36, 42
Widdemer, Margaret 97, 122
Wilcox, Ella Wheeler 84
Wilkinson, Florence 23
Wilkinson, Marguerite 21

INDEX OF AUTHORS

PART TWO

ADAMS, LÉONIE 138
AKINS, ZOË 140

BENSON, STELLA 186
BOGAN, LOUISE 154, 162

CLEGHORN, SARAH N. 149
CONKLING, GRACE HAZARD 171
CORNFORD, FRANCES 185

DAVIS, FANNIE STEARNS 191
DEUTSCH, BABETTE 196

H. D. 176, 201
HOYT, HELEN 130, 189

KENYON, BERNICE LESBIA 183
KILMER, ALINE 137, 170

LOWELL, AMY 161

MANSFIELD, KATHERINE 199
MEEKER, MARJORIE 148
MEW, CHARLOTTE 134, 166
MILLAY, EDNA ST. VINCENT . . . 133, 152, 204

O'NEILL, ROSE 160
OSTENSO, MARTHA 175

Index of Authors — Part Two

Reese, Lizette Woodworth 144
Ridge, Lola 163
Rittenhouse, Jessie B. 147
Ritter, Margaret Tod 145

Sackville, Lady Margaret 135
Seiffert, Marjorie Allen 168
Sitwell, Edith 143
Skinner, Constance Lindsay 202
Speyer, Leonora 182
Stuart, Muriel 155, 165
Swartz, Roberta Teale 164

Taggard, Genevieve 167, 173
Tietjens, Eunice 146

Untermeyer, Jean Starr 205

Warner, Sylvia Townsend 151
Welles, Winifred 172
Widdemer, Margaret 159
Wilkinson, Marguerite 188
Wylie, Elinor 131, 139, 197